SUCCESSFUL
PUBLISHING
IN SCHOLARLY
JOURNALS

SURVIVAL SKILLS FOR SCHOLARS

Managing Editor: Mitchell Allen

Survival Skills for Scholars provides you, the professor or advanced graduate student working in a college or university setting, with practical suggestions for making the most of your academic career. These brief, readable guides will help you with skills that you are required to master as a college professor but may have never been taught in graduate school. Using hands-on, jargon-free advice and examples, forms, lists, and suggestions for additional resources, experts on different aspects of academic life give invaluable tips on man- aging the day-to-day tasks of academia—effectively and efficiently.

Volumes in This Series

1. **Improving Your Classroom Teaching**
   by Maryellen Weimer

2. **How to Work With the Media**
   by James Alan Fox & Jack Levin

3. **Developing a Consulting Practice**
   by Robert O. Metzger

4. **Tips for Improving Testing and Grading**
   by John C. Ory & Katherine E. Ryan

5. **Coping With Faculty Stress**
   by Walter H. Gmelch

6. **Confronting Diversity Issues on Campus**
   by Benjamin P. Bowser, Gale S. Auletta, & Terry Jones

7. **Effective Committee Service**
   by Neil J. Smelser

8. **Getting Tenure**
   by Marcia Lynn Whicker, Jennie Jacobs Kronenfeld, & Ruth Ann Strickland

9. **Improving Writing Skills: Memos, Letters, Reports, and Proposals**
   by Arthur Asa Berger

10. **Getting Your Book Published**
    by Christine S. Smedley, Mitchell Allen & Associates

11. **Successful Publishing in Scholarly Journals**
    by Bruce A. Thyer

SURVIVAL SKILLS FOR SCHOLARS

SUCCESSFUL PUBLISHING IN SCHOLARLY JOURNALS

BRUCE A. THYER

SAGE Publications
International Educational and Professional Publisher
Thousand Oaks   London   New Delhi

For information address:

SAGE Publications, Inc.
2455 Teller Road
Thousand Oaks, California 91320

SAGE Publications Ltd.
6 Bonhill Street
London EC2A 4PU
United Kingdom

SAGE Publications India Pvt. Ltd.
M-32 Market
Greater Kailash I
New Delhi 110 048 India

Printed in the United States of America

Library of Congress Cataloging-in-Publication Data

Thyer, Bruce A.
    Successful publishing in scholarly journals/author, Bruce A. Thyer.
        p. cm.—(Survival skills for scholars; vol. 11)
    Includes bibliographical references and index.
    ISBN 0-8039-4836-0 (cl.)—ISBN 0-8039-4837-9 (pb)
        1. Scholarly periodicals—Publishing—United States. 2. Learning and scholarship—United States—Authorship. 3. Authorship—Marketing. I. Title. II. Series.
    Z479.T55   1994
    070.5'94—dc20   93-45271
                                                                       CIP

94 95 96 97 98 10 9 8 7 6 5 4 3 2 1

Sage Production Editor: Yvonne Könneker

Contents

Preface   vii

1. The Importance of Publishing Journal Articles   1
   Why Are Journal Articles
      Accorded More Weight?   2
   Why You Should Publish in Journals   5
   Summary   11

2. Selecting an Appropriate Journal   12
   Is the Journal Suitable?   12
   Does It Use Blind Peer Review?   14
   No-Fee, Subsidy, and Vanity Presses   17
   Abstracting Service Considerations   19
   Citation Indices   21
   Is the Journal Cited Much?   25
   What Is the Journal's Rejection Rate?   27
   What About Multiple Submissions?   30
   Does the Journal Have Many Subscribers?   31
   Does the Journal Treat
      Potential Authors Professionally?   32
   Is the Journal Prestigious?   33
   Do You Have Inside Information?   34
   How to Find Out More About Journals   34
   Summary   35

3. Preparing and Submitting the Manuscript   39
   Locate and Become Familiar
      With Authors' Guidelines   40

Preparing the Manuscript   40
Submitting the Manuscript   46
What About Word Processing?   49

4. Writing a Revision and Reviving a Rejection   51
How to Handle Requests for Revisions   51
What to Do
   With a Rejected Manuscript?   55
Summary   62

5. What to Do After Your Manuscript Has Been Accepted   63
Dealing With Editors   63
Returning the Completed Author's Agreement   64
Preparing Camera-Ready Figures   69
Editing Proofs   69
Ordering Reprints   75
Paying Publication Fees   76

6. Marketing Your Published Article   77
Send Your Work to Colleagues   77
Send Your Work to the Mass Media   78
Respond to Requests for Reprints   83
Provide Others With
   Your Raw Data, if Requested   84
Grant Requests to Reprint Your Work   86

7. Developing a Personal Program of Productive Publishing   88
Consider Collaboration   88
Consider Alternative
   Publication Options   100
Summary   113
Concluding Remarks   113

Appendix   115
Selected Disciplinary Writing Style Guides   115
Selected Disciplinary Journal Guides   118

References   123

About the Author   127

Preface

One of the joys of writing is sitting down after the book is completed and composing the preface. My earnest hope in preparing this monograph is to provide you, the reader, with some helpful tips and suggestions intended to make your venture into the world of publishing in scholarly journals a successful one. Novice writers will find explanations for many of the mysteries inherent in the journal publication game (and to some extent it *is* a game, as well as being a serious scholarly enterprise) and be encouraged to undertake the preparation and submission of a series of articles. Experienced writers may learn of some tactics intended to promote the development of a more productive career as a publishing scholar.

This book is not about how to write articles or how to do research. I assume that as a faculty member or practicing academic you already know these things. What it is about is how to maximize the chances that your work will eventually be accepted in a respectable journal, and how to learn about and select from the many available journal choices. It also presents some ideas on how to take advantage of the multiple (perhaps hidden) opportunities that come your way that can be turned into some form of a publication.

I have deliberately tried to write in a casual style, much as I would express myself in having a conversation with a colleague over a beer. I trust that this will not offend but will make the reading more enjoyable for you. In some places I have been dismayingly honest about the mercenary motives that can underlie one's publication efforts. It would be dishonest to pretend that these do not exist. At the same time I hope I have conveyed the seriousness with which I view the obligation of academics, and to some extent practitioners, to contribute to the knowledge base of one's discipline through publishing in scholarly journals. That this is not a completely altruistic and apolitical process should come as a surprise to no one.

I would like to acknowledge the helpful assistance of the many faculty, practitioner, and student colleagues over the years who so ably collaborated with me on various projects that resulted in journal publications. Dr. Joe Crim, Professor of Zoology at the University of Georgia, provided constructive criticism and many helpful suggestions toward improving the manuscript.

This book is lovingly dedicated to my grandmother, Maggie Thyer, former faculty member at the Cicero College of Commerce, who passed away in 1992 following a long and distinguished career as an educator and mentor to many.

1 | The Importance of Publishing Journal Articles

Publishing a volume of verse is like dropping a rose-petal down the Grand Canyon and waiting for the echo.
—Don Marquis, *The Sun Dial*

As a faculty member in an institution of higher education, graduate training, or a professional school, you probably accede to the obligation that you should be a *productive scholar*, a term that typically involves preparing some form of enduring contribution to the knowledge base of your field. Whether you are a faculty member in a department of humanities or in a medical school, a chemist or a historian, a professor of social work or of forestry, by virtue of assuming positions as teachers and scholars in institutions of higher learning, you as faculty acknowledge that the intellectual advancement of their disciplines rests heavily on their shoulders.

Many venues are available for you to make such contributions to scholarship, including the writing or editing of books, writing book chapters and monographs, delivering papers at learned societies, providing innovative lectures to your students and to other members of the university community, serving as a reviewer of works submitted for publication, writing reviews of books, preparing articles for professional newsletters, and publishing editorials and commentary related to current issues in your field.

Although there are a number of such options from which to choose, the type of contribution that is usually seen as the most significant you can make to advance the knowledge base of your field is the *peer-reviewed journal article*. There are a number of reasons for this preference, which will be outlined below.

Why Are Journal Articles Accorded More Weight?

A professional journal that uses peer review sends out all manuscripts that have been submitted to it to several scholars with presumptive expertise in the subject matter of the article. These experts give the article a thorough review and return a recommendation to the journal's editor, usually in one of three forms: Accept this work; ask the author to undertake some revisions (described) and then publish it; or reject this work. If there is clear consensus on the part of the reviewers, the journal editor is in a better position to make a decision regarding the disposition of the manuscript than if relying solely on his or her own impressions. No one editor possesses thoroughly comprehensive knowledge about all aspects of one's field, and through the use of peer review, it is hoped that the very best articles will be selected for publication and the less worthy passed over for this honor (at least in theory). Other types of scholarly contributions most often lack this type of rigorous screening process, and publication of one's works in the best journals in one's field denotes that external and independent scholars with expertise in the paper's subject matter have found merit in it. This is not to say that meritorious contributions cannot be found in books, lectures, professional papers, and the like (see Nederhof, 1989, for a strong defense of the value of books and chapters), only that the peer-review process used by most scholarly journals adds an element of confidence that such publications are valuable. It is also not to say that the journal publication system is a perfect one; indeed, it has many limitations, some of which will be discussed later on in this book. Rather, for better or worse, journal articles have been and are likely to remain for the foreseeable future the sine qua non of academic scholarly attainment (see Seiler, 1989).

Most scholarly journals can been viewed as *archival* data sources. Apart from individual subscriptions, many institutional libraries will retain these journals on their shelves for decades where the journals' accessibility to future generations of researchers is relatively easy and virtually guaranteed. If your own institutional library does not possess the journal you require, interlibrary loan facilities can place it in your hands within a few days. This aspect of *public accessibility* is a feature of journal articles that contributes to making them a more valuable contribution to the knowledge base of a discipline than classroom lectures, papers read before professional meetings, newsletter articles, and the like.

Another aspect of journal articles that sets them apart from other forms of scholarly contributions is their *self-correcting nature*. An article published in a journal is eagerly examined by hoards of jealous peers, each anxious to find mistakes in your work! If such are found, your rivals can submit responses to your article for publication in the journal your work appeared in, and you can prepare rebuttals, all available for present and future researchers to examine. Eventually, it is hoped, truth will emerge from this process. A recent example of this is the so-called cold-fusion experiments. Publication of the initial report of this phenomenon, in the respectable *Journal of Electroanalytical Chemistry and Interfacial Electrochemistry* by Stanley Pons and Martin Fleischmann, unleashed a hoard of excited scientists attempting to replicate the amazing finding that more energy could be gotten out of a test tube than was put into it. Journals grew fat with reports of apparent replications, skeptical responses, reports of alternative explanations for the researchers' original findings, and, more and more often, failures to replicate. Regrettably, the cold hard fact emerged that cold fusion was a bust (see reviews and chronological summaries of these events by Close, 1991, and by Huizenga, 1992).

Also in recent years the prestigious British journal *Nature* contained a French account of so-called polywater—a phenomenon wherein if water with extremely small amounts of a chemical agent is successively diluted, even to the point that not a single molecule of the original contaminant is likely to remain, the water appears to retain some form of "memory" of the original substance, a point maintained by homeopathic physicians for decades as the basis for the purported therapeutic efficacy of homeopathic medicine. Like cold fusion, the polywater phenomenon proved elusive; this "discovery" has been discarded. If not victories for the scientists' discovery of cold fusion or polywater, these episodes are victories for scientific truth as well as a good illustration of the self-corrective nature of the journal article publication system. These examples illustrate that the peer-review system employed by most journals acts as a brake to the injudicious dissemination of faulty scholarship, at least in the long run. As put by one retired physicist: "The purpose of refereed publication is to ensure that the paper gives all the essential details of an experiment so that others can duplicate it. If an experiment cannot be duplicated, then it cannot be trusted" (Rothman, 1990, p. 166).

Here is another benefit. The January 1993 issue of the *Proceedings of the American Mathematical Society* contained a paper called "The Mountain Climbers' Problem" describing a "new" proof of an old problem as reported by a graduate student in Budapest. Reader feedback led the dismayed Hungarian to an identical proof developed by a Japanese mathematician that had appeared in an obscure journal in 1952, over 40 years earlier! There is obviously some virtue, at least from the perspective of Tatsuo Homma in Japan, author of the original report, of journal publications determining priority of discovery (see Cripa, 1993). Related to this, the author of an original article may uncover an error in data collection or analysis and submit a corrective notice for publication in the journal him- or herself, which is another positive attribute of publishing in a journal.

Not to be overlooked (although it most often is) is the *teaching* aspect of publishing in a professional journal. Your article reaches an audience of hundreds, if not thousands, of readers who may learn something valuable from the work, a work that will patiently wait on the library shelf until needed. Scholars in other countries who learn about your article can write to you for reprints, expanding the impact of your efforts, and particularly good quality works are often included in "coursepacks" or reading lists for graduate or undergraduate courses or may be selected to appear in edited collections of readings on a particular subject, again contributing to the "teaching" elements of publishing in journals. Such benefits usually do not accompany presenting a paper at a professional meeting, delivering a sterling lecture to students, or writing a brilliant exposition for a nonarchival newsletter, further illustrating some of the superiority enjoyed by journal articles in the academic pecking order of the hen house of scholarship.

Why *You* Should Publish in Journals

There are a number of reasons that a faculty member or practicing professional like you should undertake the writing and publication of journal articles, as opposed to other forms of scholarly publication. Here are a few of them.

Promote Scholarship/Serve Humanity

The very essence of scholarship is the dissemination of knowledge for the advancement of humanity. In some instances, such as in medicine or engineering, the benefits are obvious and immediate, as when a cure is discovered for a disease, or improvements made in computational technology. For other disciplines or in the more basic sciences, new knowledge may seem of little practical value in the near future, but only time can tell the possible long-term benefits. An anthropological observation of some remote tribe's resistance to a particular disease may prove the impetus 30 years later for the discovery of some new medication. I once served on a search committee for a new dean of graduate studies, and one candidate's area of expertise was Germanic heraldry of the Middle Ages. Although such scholarly efforts may have little obvious practical value, such efforts do contribute to the humanities, without which all the technical knowledge in the world indeed would prove to be sterile and uninspiring.

One can never predict what will prove of eventual value. Who would have thought that Ivan Pavlov's work on the conditioning of gastric secretions in dogs would yield effective methods to reduce the pain of childbirth? Yet we can read that "in 1959, Dr. Lamaze, a French physician, witnessed the breathing and focusing techniques used by Russian physicians to minimize pain during childbirth. Their techniques, derived from the theory of conditioned reflexes of Dr. Ivan Pavlov, eliminated the need for heavy medication" (Novak, 1988, p. ii). Another illustration is how the family-maintained genealogical records of the Amish have proven invaluable in tracing the genetic links of certain diseases. Such examples linking initially unrelated fields with subsequent practical improvements in human affairs are both numerous and unpredictable.

Promote Your Department

Individual academic departments and professional schools receive recognition as centers of scholarly productivity in direct proportion to the degree that their faculty appear within the pages of professional journals. Indeed, a minor industry has arisen that consists of counting the number of times a given department or school appears as an institutional affiliation of its published authors. Often, various departments or schools are *ranked*, and great play is made of these rankings by the leading schools. For example, Niemi (1988) prepared a ranking study based on such research productivity for American business schools, based on a sample of outstanding business journals published between 1975 and 1985. Analogous studies can be found for psychology (e.g., Howard, Cole, & Maxwell, 1987), social work (Thyer & Bentley, 1986), sociology (Wanderer, 1966), and many other disciplines. Chairperson, deans, and directors of programs quickly bring to the attention of their administrative superiors newly published ranking studies that show their particular programs to be highly rated, and such findings can be used as leverage in the academic poker game to justify further resources (e.g., new faculty lines, graduate funding, computer equipment). Outstanding faculty and talented students are often attracted to such highly ranked departments and those lower on the ranking totem pole are in greater danger of experiencing cutbacks or outright elimination. Back in the early 1980s, when I was a graduate student at the University of Michigan, it was the lower ranked Department of Geography that was eliminated as a budget-cutting move, not the highly rated Department of Psychology.

Promote Your Career

Virtually all standards for promotion and tenure include scholarly productivity as an important element in determining whether or not a candidate shall be advanced up the academic hierarchy. Although scholarship, excellence in teaching, and professional service are presumably equally weighed in the process, the reality is that scholarship is accorded far more importance in most schools. Faculty know this, it seems. In one study, faculty at a midwest university were asked to rate how much teaching and scholarly productivity were rewarded at their school. On a 1 (not rewarded) to 5 (very well rewarded) scale, these faculty rated scholarly activity as a 4.0, teaching excellence as a 2.8, and professional service as a 2.9 (advising rated lowest at 2.1!). Such perceptions are probably accurate, given that deans and university administrators appear to endorse such views themselves (Euster & Weinbach, 1983).

Having served on a number of departmental and universitywide promotion and tenure committees, I know that a candidate's publication record is more readily quantifiable than excellence in teaching or in service. The raw numbers of publications can be counted, as can the frequency with which other scholars cite a candidate's prior work, as assessed through, for examples, the *Social Science Citation Index,* the *Science Citation Index,* or the *Index Medicus* (see Chapter 2). Committee members with a touch of masochism can undertake to read the candidate's publications and, even in the absence of substantive expertise in the candidate's discipline, gain some sense of his or her writing and research abilities. Within academic disciplines and professions, there are groups of scholars who publish articles that rank *journals themselves,* not just departments, and such lists can be consulted by academic review panels to ascertain the scholarly weights of the journals one publishes in. Such journal-based scholarly attainment can and does serve as a common denominator across disciplines within the university or college environment, hence for good or ill are accorded disproportionate weight.

On one promotion appeals committee I served with, a faculty member seeking promotion to full professor on the basis of his ocarina performances (the story is true, the instrument has been changed to protect the innocent) was turned down, despite the contention of the music department that his virtuosity as an ocarina player ("One of the top 10 ocarina players in the United States!") and his compositions were somehow comparable to journal publications. The stone-faced appeals committee was not moved by this argument, judging that the faculty member should have nevertheless produced a modicum of articles in scholarly music journals. The Shakespearian actor seeking promotion to full professor was denied for similar reasons. Do not make the mistake of modeling your academic career after that of Joe Papp, the Broadway producer, who was a full professor at Florida State University, or of Jimmy Carter at Emory, or of Dean Rusk at Georgia. Such individuals are clearly the exception to the rule. The aspiring scholar is thus well advised to develop a respectable track record in the domain of scholarship, and, for the reasons outlined previously, a considerable proportion of one's publications should take the form of peer-reviewed journal articles.

On a more mercenary level, publishing journal articles can be said to "pay off" for the academic. In one slightly tongue-in-cheek analysis, Kirk and Corcoran (an academic social worker and a lawyer) provided the following scenario:

> To illustrate the effect of publishing on an individual's career earnings, consider an assistant professor with 25 years of a career ahead. Over those 25 years, a published article that earns an initial 1-percent merit raise would result in more than $12,800. If the assistant professor publishes one article every other year and received a 1-percent merit raise for each, the financial value of the 13 articles over the 25-year career is more than $97,400. A more ambitious author in an institution that values publishing would do considerably better. (Kirk & Corcoran, 1989, p. 380)

Such figures fail to take into account the positive impact of these augmented salaries on one's retirement pay, which would further boost the value of a publication. A sophisticated empirical study by Diamond (1986) found that for a faculty member with no prior publications the "value of a citation [in 1984 dollars] to a nonfirst-author article is $314 while that of a citation to a first-author source is $402" (p. 210). It goes without saying that these figures apply primarily to publications appearing in peer-reviewed journals. Book chapters, books, monographs, book reviews, and the like are useful scholarly contributions but in general are accorded neither the attention nor the value ascribed to journal articles.

Now the merits of this state of affairs have been and are being vigorously debated within and without the academy. The relationship of research experience to quality of teaching, the value of journal publications as indices of scholarly contributions, the pressure to produce larger numbers of less valuable works, the squeezing out of the academy of dedicated instructors who devote a large amount of individualized attention to students, the avoidance of conducting investigations into "risky" areas—these are all worthy considerations in the debate.

What does seem obvious is that those who particularly value journal publication seem to be in the ascendant, and increasingly rigorous (or at least quantitative) standards of scholarly publishing are being expected of aspiring faculty, particularly among those employed at the larger universities. Like it or not, my own field is probably representative. A couple of decades ago, many faculty in schools of social work were individuals who moved into teaching after several decades of practice experience. These were most often persons with master's degrees, and holders of doctorates were rare. Promotion was earned primarily via one's excellence in teaching and university/community service. Over time the doctorate became increasingly important to the point that today it is virtually impossible to hire a new assistant professor who lacks one, no matter how talented a teacher or experienced a practitioner. Still, promotion was possible based almost solely on teaching and service. Gradually, more rigorous standards of scholarship have exerted their grip, to the point now that recent doctoral graduates are advised to have several actual articles published or in press to be competitive in the academic marketplace. My own doctoral students have lately been graduating with four to five journal article authorships already listed on their curricula vitae (CVs), a distinct professional advantage over their less published peers.

Summary

Here we have at least four reasons to publish the results of one's scholarship in professional journals: (a) to advance one's field, (b) to promote one's academic department or school, (c) to benefit oneself academically, and (d) to gain financial benefits. Left out of this analysis is any discussion of a fifth reason, the intrinsic rewards of journal publishing. Included could be such variables as the joys of writing as a professional activity. There is the warm glow of seeing one's work appear in the very best journals, responding to requests for reprints, and engaging in subsequent stimulating correspondence with one's colleagues. Benjamin Franklin said, "Nothing gives an author so much pleasure as to find his works respectfully quoted by other learned authors." While this may be a bit of an exaggeration, certainly being cited by others is an enjoyable experience, perhaps equalled by being invited (on the basis of one's superb scholarship) to give invited addresses at professional meetings. Although not readily quantifiable, such factors are very real and cannot be ignored.

Now, having thoroughly persuaded you of the great importance there is in publishing your work in scholarly journals, let us discuss the nuts and bolts of selecting a suitable journal to publish your article.

2 | Selecting an Appropriate Journal

If you don't know where you want to go, you might wind up someplace else.

—Satchel Paige

By the time one has become an assistant professor in a college or university, professional socialization has usually made the budding scholar aware of which journals in a given field may be considered among the best or most reputable. Generally speaking, the higher the rejection rate of a given journal, the more prestigious it is seen to be. In selecting from the available journal outlets, authors should ask themselves a series of questions that are useful in determining the most suitable home for their work.

Is the Journal Suitable?

For academics, the most prestigious journals are generally those that are seen as *research* journals, those that publish the results of serious scholarly inquiry. Across disciplines the question of what constitutes serious scholarly inquiry can vary widely. For some fields, such as philosophy or psychoanalysis, the requisites are a thorough familiarity with prior work in a given area, together with some original intellectual contributions of one's own. For others, such as medicine, the epitome of scholarly research consists of authoring a large scale, multisite, international, controlled clinical trial of some new lifesaving drug. Originality, per se, or creative thought may be completely absent from the publication. An archeologist may fruitfully publish a lengthy work based on a small fragment of pottery, a behavior analyst a controlled inquiry based on a single client, a chemist the molecular structure of a new compound, and an epidemiologist the results of a large-scale investigation of the prevalence of a particular disease on a single continent. The point is that the question of what constitutes acceptable scholarship varies widely across disciplines, and such standards are reflected in academic journals within and across disciplines.

For example, take the case of psychiatry. The *Archives of General Psychiatry* is more oriented toward the production of large-scale group research, and an extensive clinical history-type of article would not be well received. However, any of a number of psychoanalytic journals would be delighted to publish such case histories. Within psychology, the *Journal of Consulting and Clinical Psychology* typically publishes the results of group outcome studies and does not publish single-subject experimental designs very frequently. However, the *Journal of Applied Behavior Analysis* publishes single-subject experimental research almost exclusively, and group outcome studies rarely darken its pages.

Some journals are oriented toward a particular theoretical focus or conceptual framework; others are clearly eclectic. Hence an early issue for the academic seeking an outlet for a manuscript is to determine the suitability of the manuscript's subject matter, theoretical base, and methodology (perhaps even the outcome) for a particular journal. For example, a controlled outcome study that demonstrates that psychoanalytic psychotherapy did not help clients may find a friendlier home in a behavioral journal than in a mainstream psychoanalytic one. A study showing that behavior therapy was of greater benefit to clinically depressed persons than antidepressant medication might be more favorably viewed by the editorial board of a psychology journal than one devoted to biological psychiatry. Use the rough guide of determining in which journals related research has been published, and consider submitting your work to one or more of those outlets. Titles alone can be misleading. The *Journal of Applied Behavior Analysis* and the *Journal of Applied Behavioral Science* both deal with the same broad subject matter, human behavior, but there is virtually no overlap in the types of articles published, in terms of either methodology or conceptual frameworks.

Not to be overlooked, particularly in some professions such as medicine, are *practice* journals. These outlets are not devoted to publishing original reports of newly discovered knowledge as much as they are designed to convey to practitioners information about techniques or methods that have been empirically established as effective that practitioners may find useful. In the hierarchy of academia, articles published in practice journals are generally held in lower esteem than those appearing in research journals, but this may vary across fields.

Does It Use Blind Peer Review?

Perhaps the most important consideration in choosing a journal to submit your article to is whether or not it selects articles on the basis of peer review. In this approach, a manuscript is received by the editor, who sends it out to two or more individuals with expertise in the subject matter of your paper. After some time, ranging from 2 weeks to several months, these reviewers send in critical commentary and a recommendation to the editor with respect to your article. The editor assimilates these reviews and uses them to assist in making a decision about the disposition of the work. Again, speaking generally, journals that make use of peer review are held in considerably greater esteem than those that do not. There are a very few exceptions. For example, the prestigious *Behavioral and Brain Sciences* published by Oxford University Press actively solicits lengthy manuscripts from well-established scientists. Rather than undergoing peer review, the editor arranges for a number of other specialists in a given field to prepare critical commentary about the lead article, then publishes the article, numerous commentaries about it, and then the original author's response to these comments—all in one issue of the journal. But such practices are the exception, rather than the rule, and authors (particularly those in the initial stages of their careers) should primarily seek to publish in peer-reviewed journals.

A further dimension in the peer-review process is whether or not the reviews are provided "blindly." There are at least two forms in which blind review can be undertaken. In the first, the authors' names and affiliations are removed from the manuscript when it is sent to reviewers for their evaluation. Some feel that by using this form of blind review, with the reviewers presumably not aware of the authors' identities or institutional affiliations, the potential for bias is reduced. For example, if a leading expert is known to have written a particular article, a reviewer may be less appropriately critical than would otherwise be the case. Or, if a relative unknown authored a manuscript, reviewers might tend to be harsher. An article written by someone from the Harvard Medical School may be treated differently than one from the Medical College of Georgia, hence the accepted practice of removing such information from manuscripts.

Although the concept of blind peer review has some intuitive appeal, it is not clear to what extent it actually helps the process be more objective. Sometimes informed reviewers can infer the authors' identity from the subject matter of the paper or other subtle indicators. However, many of the very best journals use blind review conducted in this manner, while others, also among the very best, do not. In general, this issue should not weigh heavily in journal selection by the prospective author because a journal's reputation is primarily established by the overall quality of the material it publishes, not so much by the mechanism used in reviewing and selecting articles for publication.

Blind review may also be undertaken in a second form, in which reviews are blind only to the extent that the authors of a submitted manuscript do not know the identities of those serving as peer reviewers of their work. In such cases, the reviewers *do* know the authors' identities and affiliations. This latter form of blind review is more characteristic of journals in the so-called "hard sciences," with the former type more often associated with the behavioral and social sciences.

Peer review, whether conducted blindly or not, is itself no guarantee of a bias-free process. A small industry has grown up around the problems and pitfalls of peer-reviewing practices and of editorial decision making. In a survey of more than 500 reviews provided by a number of psychology journals, Spencer, Hartnett, and Mahoney (1985) found considerable evidence of emotional persuasion and unanchored commentary, indicative of biases and prejudices in the review process. In a clever and landmark study in the area, Peters and Ceci (1982) submitted articles that had been recently published in leading psychology journals *back to* the same journal that published the article, retyped, and with unknown author names and obscure institutional affiliations. A large proportion of these resubmitted but already published works were turned down as not suitable for publication, often because of purportedly serious methodological considerations! This is a crude approximation of what psychometric specialists call test-retest reliability, and in many instances it appears to be rather low. Related to this, Scott (1974) found a considerable amount of disagreement among reviewers of the same manuscript, related to what is known as interrater reliability (see also Eberley & Warner, 1990; Hargens, 1988). Cullen and Macauley (1992) demonstrate that close consistency is indeed possible to achieve among reviewers, which is a somewhat comforting thought.

Even if blind peer review is used, a journal editor has a considerable amount of latitude in making a decision about a manuscript. In dealing with one controversial manuscript submitted by this writer, the editor of the journal I submitted it to sent it to a total of *nine* reviewers and asked me to deal with all of their concerns and issues in preparing a revision, if I cared to make one. In another, the initial set of reviewers' comments were relatively favorable, but the journal editor did not care for my work so she sent the manuscript out again for further reviews, this time selecting as reviewers individuals the editor knew shared her biases. Of course, editors are not bound, in any event, to abide by the recommendations of reviewers.

The point of all this is that authors submitting work to a scholarly journal should be under no illusions that their work will be treated in a completely objective, bias-free manner. Some field's journals are slanted in favor of positive findings (e.g., Epstein, 1990), while others tend to discount replication research (e.g., Neuliep & Crandell, 1993). The journal publication system, even among those journals using blind peer review, is fraught with pitfalls. Lindsey (1978) provides a dated but still instructive review of studies of the peer-review procedures used by journals to select articles for publication, and Cicchetti's (1991) study is a more up-to-date treatment of the subject. In the absence of reasonable alternatives, however, peer review, particularly when conducted blindly, remains the best approach among a range of less desirable options. I tend to concur with the views of Cullen and Macauley (1992), who note that "although peer review systems are imperfect and require constant oversight, many consider them to be the best mechanism yet conceived to systematically evaluate scientific material" (p. 859).

No-Fee, Subsidy, and Vanity Presses

Although this varies by discipline, it is the practice of most scholarly journals *not* to charge authors any fees to publish their works. This is particularly true in the social and behavioral sciences and the humanities. Often, however, especially among the "bench-science" journals (e.g., chemistry, physics), it is customary and acceptable to charge a publication fee to the authors of accepted works.

In general, if it is not the common practice to employ a publication charge in a given discipline, the author should avoid those that do exact such a fee. Such charges are most often levied by the less rigorous journals (those with higher acceptance rates), and they take on the characteristic of basically being paid to publish work.

There are a number of permutations to this process, and the field of psychology will be used to illustrate it. The very best journals, such as those published by the American Psychological Association, use blind peer review and do not assess publication fees of any type. Authors have the *option* to purchase professionally typeset reprints of their work at the time of publication. Within the general field of psychology though, journals may be found that exact a *mandatory* fee to publish an article, usually based on the number of typeset pages for a given article. These can be quite high. A journal that charges a $50 per page fee collects $500 from the authors of a 10-page article. Such journals are suspiciously akin to subsidy book presses, which undertake to publish your book-length manuscript in return for a substantial fee. Just as books produced by subsidy presses are generally considered less credible than those published by the larger proprietary publishing houses or university presses, journals that charge the author a printing charge, *for those disciplines in which this is not the common practice*, are generally less rigorous and less "merit" accrues to the author of such articles.

A variation on this is to have a *mandatory* reprint purchase policy, wherein the journal does not charge for the publication of an article per se, but the authors are "required" (as a condition of publication) to purchase a minimum number of reprints (e.g., 200), for which a similarly large fee is charged. A small number of (sometimes) less prestigious journals have a *submission fee*, wherein authors must provide a fee ($10-$25), up front, to cover the costs of processing their article by the journal, with no guarantee of acceptance.

Journals employing one or more of these practices are best avoided by an author, *unless* such is the common practice in the author's field (e.g., the "hard" sciences), in which case it is perfectly acceptable (the rationale here is that most research is these fields is supported through external funding, which makes publication fees available). My own bias is to try to get an article published in a mainstream journal, and if, after a number of attempts, I have been unable to find a home for it, then to submit it to a subsidy press journal. I console myself with noting the names of some of the leading persons in psychology who occasionally publish in these types of journals. Even if peer review is less stringent and a fee is assessed, at least my work is available in an archival source and my research/writing is not a total write-off. The downside is that most of my colleagues are aware of the lower quality of these subsidy journals, and articles appearing in such outlets are accorded less merit. It is a particularly bad practice, if one is coming up for promotion or tenure, to have a large number of subsidy journal publications on one's vitae. Such articles will typically not help the candidate and may promote the reputation that he or she produces low-quality scholarship incapable of appearing in the best journals.

Abstracting Service Considerations

Most of the academic disciplines and practice professions have some form of abstracting service that is relevant to their fields. These are journal-style publications that are periodically updated (monthly, quarterly, etc.) and contain complete citations and abstracts of journal articles recently published in that field. A selected number (but by no means all) of these abstracting periodicals are listed in Table 2.1.

These services serve students and scholars by bringing together a précis of recent work in one small publication, so that scholars do not have to comb through all the journals that may carry work of interest to them. Take, for example, *Psychological Abstracts* (*PA*), published by the American Psychological Association. A researcher interested in, say, the topic of "behavior therapy" could look up the most recent issue of *PA*, turn to the heading of "behavior therapy," and find complete citations and abstracts for all articles published related to that theme for a selected time period (usually 3

Table 2.1 Selected Major Abstracting Services

Abstracts in Social Gerontology (journal published by Sage Periodicals Press)

Aquatic Sciences and Fisheries Abstracts (Cambridge Scientific Abstracts)

Chemical Abstracts (weekly periodical published by the American Chemical Society)

Communication Abstracts (Sage journal)

Educational Administration Abstracts (Corwin Press journal)

Human Resources Abstracts (Sage journal)

Journal of Planning Literature (Sage journal)

PsychSCAN: Developmental Psychology (APA journal)

PsychSCAN: Clinical Psychology (APA journal)

SAGE Family Studies Abstracts (Sage journal)

SAGE Public Administration Abstracts (Sage journal)

SAGE Race Relations Abstracts (Sage, London, journal)

SAGE Urban Studies Abstracts (Sage journal)

Psychological Abstracts (APA periodical)

Social Work Research and Abstracts (quarterly journal published by the NASW Press)

Sociological Abstracts (American Sociological Society periodical)

---

months). The researcher could examine these abstracts and note the citations of those of interest, and subsequently look them up manually or arrange for a graduate assistant, helper, or library service to obtain copies of the actual articles. Many abstracting services are prepared in a CD-ROM format and can be accessed either by going to the library or remotely. Convenient printers may allow you to obtain a record of the complete citation and abstract immediately. By having one's work appear in a journal that is reviewed by a major abstracting service, the chances that it will come to the attention of other scholars who make use of it are greatly enhanced.

As an author, you are interested in maximizing the amount of coverage your article receives. My bottom-line recommendation is that you opt to send your manuscripts to journals abstracted by one or more of the major abstracting services, in lieu of sending them to journals that are not so abstracted. Generally speaking, abstracting services do not include a journal for review until it is well established, and those that lack such abstracting features can be said to be less credible than those that do not. Information about the abstracting services that review a particular journal can usually be found in the frontispiece or copyright page of each issue of that journal, a sample of which can be found in Figure 2.1. As can be seen, articles published in *Research on Social Work Practice* (a quarterly journal that I founded and of which I serve as editor) are abstracted in *Psychological Abstracts, Current Contents, Social Work Research and Abstracts, Sociological Abstracts,* and so on. Accordingly, an author can be assured that, should her article be published in this journal, a summary of it, along with complete reference information, will appear in all these other periodicals and outlets, greatly enhancing the visibility of the work and the likelihood that others will make use of the research and cite the article.

Citation Indices

Akin to abstracting services, citation indices consist of journal-format publications that appear on a regular basis (often quarterly) and list the names of authors of articles that have appeared in the references of recent journal articles. Other versions will list articles by *topic*. Hence one could turn to the *Index Medicus* and look up all articles published in 1993 written by L. Pasteur *and/or* look up all articles listed under the topic of *rabies*, regardless of authorship. Among the more common citation indices are the *Social Science Citation Index*, the *Science Citation Index*, the *Index Medicus*, and numerous others (see Table 2.2). You probably became familiar with those relevant to your own discipline during your doctoral training. As in the case of abstracting services, an author should consider whether a given journal is reviewed

RESEARCH ON SOCIAL WORK PRACTICE is a disciplinary journal devoted to the publication of empirical research concerning the methods and outcomes of social work practice. Social work practice is broadly interpreted to refer to the application of intentionally designed social work intervention programs to problems of societal and/or interpersonal importance, including behavior analysis or psychotherapy involving individuals; case management; practice involving couples, families, and small groups; community practice and development; and implementation and evaluation of social policies.

The journal will serve as an outlet for the publication of original reports of quantitatively oriented evaluation studies on the outcomes of social work practice; reports on the development and validation of new methods of assessment for use in social work practice; empirically based reviews of the practice literature that provide direct applications to social work practice; and theoretical or conceptual papers that have direct relevance to social work practice. All empirical research articles must conform to accepted standards of conventional scientific inquiry. Articles employing either group or single-system research methodologies are equally welcome, as are manuscripts representing a variety of theoretical orientations or conceptual frameworks.

An editorial board of nationally known social workers with expertise in the principles and methodologies of practice research will provide timely and constructive reviews of each manuscript. All reviews will be conducted using blind peer-review procedures. Authors can expect an editorial decision within three months of submission. Manuscripts and an abstract should be submitted in quadruplicate to Bruce A. Thyer, Editor, **RESEARCH ON SOCIAL WORK PRACTICE**, School of Social Work, University of Georgia, Athens, Georgia 30602; (706) 542-5440. Articles should be typewritten and double-spaced, with footnotes, references, tables, and figures on separate pages. Manuscripts should follow the *Publication Manual of the American Psychological Association*, 3rd edition.

RESEARCH ON SOCIAL WORK PRACTICE (ISSN 1049-7315) is published four times annually—in January, April, July, and October—by Sage Publications, Inc., 2455 Teller Road, Thousand Oaks, CA 91320. Telephone: (805) 499-0721; FAX/Order line: (805) 499-0871. Copyright © 1993 by Sage Publications, Inc. All rights reserved. No portion of the contents may be reproduced in any form without written permission from the publisher.

Subscriptions: Regular institutional rate $113.00 per year, $29.00 single issue. Individuals may subscribe at a one-year rate of $46.00, $15.00 single issue. Add $6.00 for subscriptions outside the United States. Orders from the U.K., Europe, the Middle East, and Africa should be sent to the London address (below). Orders from India should be sent to the New Delhi address (below). Noninstitutional orders must be paid by personal check, VISA, or MasterCard.

Figure 2.1. Frontispiece or Copyright Page for the Journal *Research on Social Work Practice*

Application to mail at SECOND CLASS rate is pending at Thousand Oaks, California.

This journal is abstracted or indexed in **Research Alert, Health and Psychosocial Instrument, Psychological Abstracts, PsycINFO, Sociological Abstracts, Social Planning/Policy & Development Abstracts, Linguistics and Language Behavior Abstracts, Current Contents/Social & Behavioral Sciences, Social Sciences Citation Index,** and **Social Work Research & Abstracts.**

Back Issues: Information about availability and prices of back issues may be obtained from the publisher's order department (address below). Single-issue orders for 5 or more copies will receive a special adoption discount. Contact the order department for details. Write to the London office for sterling prices.

Inquiries: Address all correspondence and permission requests to SAGE PUBLICATIONS, Inc., 2455 Teller Road, Thousand Oaks, CA 91320. Telephone (805) 499-0721; FAX (805) 499-0871. Inquiries and subscriptions from the U.K., Europe, the Middle East, and Africa should be sent to SAGE PUBLICATIONS, Ltd., 6 Bonhill Street, London EC2A 4PU, United Kingdom. From India, write to SAGE PUBLICATIONS INDIA Pvt. Ltd., P.O. Box 4215, New Delhi 110 048 India. Other orders should be sent to the Thousand Oaks office.

Authorization to photocopy items for internal or personal use, or the internal or personal use of specific clients, is granted by Sage Publications, Inc., for libraries and other users registered with the Copyright Clearance Center (CCC) Transactional Reporting Service, provided that the base fee of 25¢ per copy, plus 10¢ per copy page, is paid directly to CCC, 21 Congress St., Salem, MA 01970. 1049-7315/93 $.25 + .10.

Advertising: Current rates and specifications may be obtained by writing to the Advertising Manager at the Thousand Oaks office (address above).

Claims: Claims for undelivered copies must be made no later than twelve months following month of publication. The publisher will supply missing copies when losses have been sustained in transit and when the reserve stock will permit.

Change of Address: Six weeks' advance notice must be given when notifying of change of address. Please send old address label along with the new address to ensure proper identification. Please specify name of journal. POSTMASTER: Send address changes to: **Research on Social Work Practice,** c/o 2455 Teller Road, Thousand Oaks, CA 91320.

Printed on acid-free paper

Figure 2.1. Continued

by the citation index relevant to his or her field. This is perhaps most important for academic authors seeking promotion or tenure.

Table 2.2 Selected Major Citation Indices

Current Contents: Social & Behavioral Sciences (Weekly journal published by the Institute for Scientific Information. Also available in six other editions, including life sciences; clinical medicine; physical, chemical, and earth sciences; agriculture, biology, and environmental sciences; engineering, technology, and applied sciences; arts and humanities. All editions except arts and humanities also available on computer diskette.)

Index Medicus (published by the National Institutes of Health, National Library of Medicine [NIH])

AIDS Bibliography (NIH)

Neuroscience Citation Index (CD-ROM database produced by the Institute for Scientific Information. This firm also produces CD-ROM databases for the fields of biochemistry and biophysics, biomedical engineering, biotechnology, chemistry, and materials science.)

Science Citation Index (Institute for Scientific Information periodical [ISI])

Social Science Citation Index (ISI periodical. Covers over 40 disciplines. Also available in CD-ROM version.)

Index to Scientific Reviews (ISI periodical)

Biological and Agricultural Index (periodical published by the H. W. Wilson Co.)

General Science Index (H. W. Wilson Co.)

Computer and Control Abstracts (published by the Institute of Electrical Engineers)

Cumulative Index to Nursing and Allied Health Literature (published by CINAHL Information Systems)

Many others

NOTE: Most of the above indices are available on CD-ROM or other on-line versions.

A measure (albeit imperfect) of the extent to which one's scholarship is useful to one's field is the number of times one's work is cited by others on a yearly basis (see Taubes, 1993). Indeed, some promotion and tenure standards now request that information on this measure be included in the candidate's dossier. Crudely put, a faculty member whose work is cited an average of 4 times a year over the past 5 years could be construed as having a smaller impact in his or her field than someone cited by others an average of 50 times a year. This calculus does not take into account variables such as the size of one's field (someone active in an obscure area of scholarship is placed at a disadvantage in the above illustration), the *quality* of one's research (a person's paper could be cited frequently as an example of poor scholarship!), or particularly controversial findings (à la Pons and Fleischmann's "discovery" of cold fusion). Nevertheless, all other factors being equal, the extent to which one's work is cited by others is a useful benchmark of scholarly impact and is widely used as one variable to be factored into the tenure and promotion decision-making process. Accordingly, seek to publish in journals that are covered by your discipline's most important citation indices.

Is the Journal Cited Much?

Apart from the issue of whether or not a given journal is listed in various citation indices is the extent to which others actually *read and cite* articles appearing in that journal. One way of assessing such impact is by consulting various disciplinary citation indices. For example, in my broad areas of research, the most relevant index is published by the Institute for Scientific Information and is called the *Social Science Journal Citation Record* (*SSJCR*; see Garfield, 1988). In the *SSJCR*, one can look up journals in various subfields and see how particular ones are "ranked" on various measures of purported scholarly value. One such indicator is the *citation number*, reflective of the number of times a given journal has been cited in a given year, by all the journals covered in the *Social Science Citation Index*.

Illustrative data are provided by Friman, Allen, Kerwin, and Larzelere (1993). In 1988 the citation number for the journal *Cognitive Psychology* was 1,707; that for *Cognition*, the lesser figure of 832. It would seem that articles appearing in *Cognitive Psychology* were more widely cited (in 1988) than those published in *Cognition*. An author considering where to send his article involving cognitive science may take such an index into account in arriving at a decision.

Of course the citation number of a journal is influenced by factors other than the intrinsic worth of the articles appearing on its pages. The mandatory-reprint-purchase-policy journal *Psychological Reports* enjoys a very high citation number, in part because it publishes dozens and dozens of articles each issue (issues have large numbers of pages and use relatively small type). Irrespective of the *quality* of these reports, their sheer number helps promote the high citation number of *Psychological Reports*. Obviously, a bimonthly journal has an advantage over a quarterly one, a monthly over a bimonthly, and a weekly over a monthly, in terms of the annual citation number.

Less influenced by the volume of articles is the *SSJCR's* *impact factor*. This is calculated, for any given year, "by dividing all citations to articles in that journal in the preceding two years by the journal's source items in the preceding two years" (Friman et al., 1993, p. 659). In other words, "the impact factor is a measure of how frequently an average article is cited in a specified year" (Friman et al., 1993, p. 659). The 1988 impact factor for *Cognitive Psychology* was 3.38, while that for *Cognition* was 2.82. Apparently the average article appearing in the former journal is cited more often than one in the latter, another potential consideration in selecting a journal to which to send one's groundbreaking new study.

The writer can consult recent volumes of the *SSJCR* (found in the reference room of your local university—an easy task given that every teacher's and A&M college has now joined the formerly elite ranks of those institutions called "universities"), look up various subdisciplines (e.g., cognitive, behavioral, psychoanalytic), and the relative rankings of that field's various journals, and obtain further data useful in selecting among possible journal choices. Similar reference books are available for disciplines unrelated to the social sciences, prepared by the Institute for Scientific Information as well as other publishers.

What Is the Journal's Rejection Rate?

In the Byzantine world of scholarly publishing, it is assumed that blind rigorous peer review of submitted manuscripts results in a weeding out of less meritorious works, permitting only the very best articles to find print in the very best journals. Accordingly, a journal's *rejection rate* (or, conversely, its acceptance rate) is a consideration in determining where to send your work. A journal with a 90% rejection rate eventually prints only 1 out of 10 articles submitted to it. Logically, it would seem that a work appearing in such an outlet typically would be of greater value (in the obscure calculus of one's individual discipline) than one accepted in a journal with a 60% rejection rate. *Science, Nature,* the *Harvard Law Review,* the *Archives of General Psychiatry,* and *The New England Journal of Medicine* are examples of high quality journals with fairly high rejection rates. Most scholars in the field of medicine, for example, would accord greater prestige to a piece of research appearing in the *Journal of the American Medical Association (JAMA)* than one in the *Journal of the Georgia Medical Association,* in part because of the former's higher rejection rate. All is not as simple as it seems, however. In some fields, very high quality journals, such as those dealing with physics, mathematics, and biochemistry, have comparatively low rejection rates, on the order of 30%-40% being turned down. Even here the basic principle still stands. The journal within a given field with the higher rejection rate, all other things being equal, will be seen as a higher quality one than those that accept more submissions.

Does this mean that you should only send your work to journals with relatively high rejection rates? No. Very often your own honest appraisal of your article tells you that it does not meet the high standards of publication in your field's leading periodicals. To submit your work to them would most likely result in an undue delay in its eventual publication, as the editor of the number one journal slowly processed it through blind review and eventually got around to informing you, regrettably, of its rejection (or, in a phrase I sometimes use to spare an author's self-esteem, "that the reviews were insufficiently positive to warrant publication")! This is demoralizing at best to the aspiring author, and such experiences often can be avoided by a judicious consideration of the appropriateness of various journals.

One of the very first articles I ever wrote was submitted to the top rank *Journal of Consulting and Clinical Psychology*, published by the American Psychological Association. The editor at the time, David Barlow, processed it promptly and sent me a carefully crafted letter of rejection—kindly worded but nonetheless a rejection. Resubmitted to the less prestigious Journal of Clinical Psychology (published by a proprietary publishing company), the article was accepted with minimal revisions. Inasmuch as I would like to believe that all my fine work deserves a place in the very best journals in the human services, realistically I know that such is not the case and I select my journals accordingly. In fact, when I initially send a manuscript off for publication, I generally have a tentative list of second-, third-, and even fourth-choice journal options stuck in the hard-copy file somewhere for future use if the article is rejected by the first choice.

Two years ago a doctoral student and I conducted a preliminary study on the content validity of a credentialing examination developed and marketed by a large professional association (let's call it "The Federation") to which I belong. Indeed, The Federation makes a large sum of money each year by administering this examination and offering the credential through testing and application fees. The results of our study cast doubt on the value of the written examination. We wrote up a report in the form of a journal article and decided to send it to The Federation's major journal, one that is sent to all members of the field. We reasoned that, given The Federation's vested interest in this test's value, they deserved first shot at publishing our study critical of it. Time passed—*lots* of time! I called the editorial office; I wrote polite letters; eventually, after more than 9 months, I visited The Federation's national headquarters (while visiting that city for an unrelated meeting) to inquire about the disposition of my article. All to no avail. Each such inquiry was met with the response: "It is being processed by the reviewers" or "We are awaiting comments from an additional reviewer." Eventually, after *14 months* of waiting, we received a letter of rejection, accompanied by two sets of reviewer's remarks, each of less than one third of a page! The same day, given the lack of substantial critical analysis in the reviewers' remarks, I sent the manuscript to a journal published by a rival professional association, one with perhaps one tenth the number of subscribers relative to the first journal we had sent it to. This number two journal also used peer review and is picked up by various citation services (my own minimal standards). The manuscript was accepted, virtually as submitted, within 2 months. If I had been realistic (as opposed to naive and idealistic), I should have foreseen that it was possible that The Federation's proprietary interests could result in the manuscript's being delayed unduly, and perhaps rejected, because its results reflected unfavorably on The Federation's prized credentialing examination. Regardless of whether these mercenary reasons influenced the editorial disposition of my manuscript (I have no way of knowing), certainly 14 months is far too long for any credible journal to take to arrive at a decision, pro or con.

I learned another valuable lesson through this experience, and so did my frustrated doctoral student. Although we would all like to take a chance on getting our work in print in the very best outlets, sometimes a reality check is necessary to avoid frustrating outcomes. Initially sending your article to a more specialized or to a lesser rated journal is sometimes an option worth considering. In doing so it is possible to shorten the time to eventual publication.

What About Multiple Submissions?

It is the convention in virtually all academic fields that one's article is submitted to only *one journal at a time*. If, and only if, it is rejected by the first journal is it permissible to submit it to a second journal. Similarly, only after it has been rejected by the second journal is it permitted to send it to journal three, and so on. This avoids having journal editorial boards processing manuscripts, perhaps devoting a large amount of time and editorial resources in providing feedback or even accepting the article, and then having authors writing to the editor to say, "Sorry, I have decided to publish it in the *Journal of Askesis* instead of your *Galimatias Gazette*. Thanks anyway for the commentary!" This would be annoying at best and result in a tremendous squandering of journal resources.

Sometimes editorial guidelines (such as those in the *Publication Manual of the American Psychological Association*) contain explicit statements prohibiting such multiple submissions, and all journals that adopt such guidelines expect the authors of submitted manuscripts to act accordingly. This can vary by discipline, however. Several years ago I served on my university's promotion and tenure review committee (the one up from departmental review), and an assistant professor in the school of law came up for review, having been recommended by the law faculty for promotion and tenure. The faculty member ("Professor Solon") had credible teaching and service accomplishments but had published only three works, including two law review articles. My committee turned down Solon's application on the grounds of insufficient scholarship. Professor Solon appealed our decision and made a personal appearance before us. He made much of the high quality of his law review articles and of the high rejection rates of these outlets. I asked him how many such journals he had had to send his articles to before having them accepted. Professor Solon told me that, with respect to law review articles, multiple submissions are acceptable, and even encouraged, and that faculty often send their articles to numerous law reviews. Apparently, to take an extreme case, if one sent a manuscript to 20 law review journals, each with a 95% rejection rate, the odds were that 1 of the 20 would accept one's article. This is what Solon had done, legal and acceptable in his field, apparently. Nice! However, such a practice takes much of the value out of apparently high rejection rates. If the *Harvard Law Review* turns you down, you still have a chance with the *Michigan Law Review*, and so on down the line. Such multiple submission practices are rare among scholarly journals. Be sure to consult the practice standards for your particular discipline or profession before engaging in multiple submissions. If in doubt, don't do it!

Does the Journal Have Many Subscribers?

Obviously you would like to have your article read by as many people in your field as possible. Accordingly, the numbers of subscribers to a given journal deserves your attention, in that the greater the number of subscribers, presumably the greater number of readers of your article. The flagship journal published by the National Association of Social Workers, *Social Work*, is sent to all members of the association, more than 140,000 professional social workers, whereas the *Journal of Applied Social Sciences* (another social work journal) has about 600 subscribers. It is clear which journal outlet is likely to provide the most readers for your article. Keep in mind, however, that many fields are relatively small, and some extremely high-quality journals have fewer than 1,000 subscribers, particularly in the hard sciences. Also, simply because a journal is sent to people does not mean that it is widely read. This is particularly true in the case of journals sent out as part of one's membership in a professional association. Many people join professional associations because of various benefits—with the hallmark journal not being one of them! The journal appears and is pitched out, relegated to a waiting room, or passed on, unread, to graduate students.

Does the Journal Treat
Potential Authors Professionally?

Journals often commit three major sins in their dealings with the authors of submitted manuscripts. The first sin is to take far too long in arriving at decisions and notifying authors about the disposition of their articles. Given the "half-life" of new knowledge in many fields, timely decision making can be crucial. Also, you may be in particular need of additional accepted articles to list in your promotion and tenure dossier, just prior to going up for review. Or you may be a practitioner attempting the leap from practice into academic life, and you wisely know that having a few articles accepted for publication will enhance your chances of being offered a faculty position.

There are two major sources for finding out about this time lag. The first, and most credible, is from your colleagues who have had experience with particular journals. Ask around and find out. The second source is to consult the various "Authors' Guides" to journals in your discipline (described below). The average time lag is often published there, based on information provided by the editor. Two caveats are in order here. First, journal editors may play loose and fast with the truth, in order to make their journal appear more attractive to potential authors, by claiming a quicker turnaround time than is realistically the case for most of their manuscripts. Second, sometimes they simply do not respond to this request, and where the phrase *review time* is listed in the authors' guide, it is left blank or says "unknown." Your colleagues are probably a more reliable source than an authors' guide.

A second dimension of responsible treatment of authors is the amount and quality of reviewer feedback that accompanies returned manuscripts. A journal editor who simply tells the author of a submitted manuscript that it was rejected, or gives some spurious excuse such as lack of journal space, and leaves it at that is nowhere as helpful as one who accompanies the rejection letter with a complete set of reviewer commentary (from blind reviews). The author can read these remarks and possibly revise the manuscript in a form more suitable for submission to another journal—in other words, develop a new and improved manuscript. This can be seen as small recompense for the author's months of waiting, only to get a rejection. Some journals to which I have submitted articles make it a routine practice to return pages and pages of single-spaced reviewers' comments and suggestions for the manuscript's improvement, even if the decision was to reject the work. This is an instructive, often invaluable, service that journals can and should provide authors, in my opinion. Seek out and publish your work in such outlets, if at all possible.

The third sin is to take too long, once an article has been accepted for publication, to have the article actually appear in print. One journal in the field of social work is notorious for taking exceptionally long in this regard, often requiring 3 to 4 years prior to publication. Authors have begun to avoid sending their work to this outlet for this reason. All other factors being equal, seek to publish in the journal with the shortest lag time from acceptance to print.

Is the Journal Prestigious?

Most often you will already have a good sense of which journals in your field are seen as the most prestigious ones to publish in. Ask around if you are unsure. For some disciplines, various quantitative and qualitative indices have been developed to *rank* journals empirically in terms of prestige (e.g., Feingold, 1989; Fry, Walters, & Schuerman, 1985; Koulack & Keselman, 1975; Lake & Doke, 1987; Peery & Adams, 1981). If such analyses have been performed for the journals in your field, consulting these may be helpful.

Do You Have Inside Information?

Sometimes you may have access to the equivalent of stock investors' "inside information" related to particular journals, which can help you select (or discard) potential choices. If your major professor (Dr. Pundit, a coauthor on your article?) was herself trained by Professor Maven, the editor of the prestigious (and mythical) *Journal of Akesis*, you might consider submitting your work to Professor Maven's journal, particularly if your major professor remains on good terms with the editor. You could insert a brief paragraph (or attach a yellow sticky note) to your submission letter extending warm greetings from Dr. Pundit to Professor Maven, via you. It cannot hurt.

If your article takes a particular slant, or is theoretically biased in a certain direction, and you have the choice of sending your work to one of two journals, obviously if the editor of one of the journals is identifiable as sharing the viewpoint of your paper then that would suggest which journal to send your work to. Similarly, if you extensively cite Professor Maven's publications in your article, and Maven is the editor of a journal that is appropriate for your work, then by all means send it to Maven.

How to Find Out More About Journals

It was estimated a few years ago that there were more than 40,000 scientific journals being published worldwide (Broad, 1988), not to mention those relevant to the humanities, arts and letters, professions, and other academic subjects. A 1991 article in the January 14 issue of *Newsweek* claimed the existence of more than 74,000 scientific journals! Thus even the best informed scholar is hard pressed to keep abreast of all of the potential publication outlets available for his or her manuscripts. It pays to wander periodically through the stacks of one's institutional library and browse through recent issues of established and newly founded journals in one's field as one means of remaining current with journal developments.

A better option is to purchase commercially available books that do nothing except contain detailed information about all the journals in a given field. Listings found in these types of books for a given journal include the journal name, publisher, editor, subscription information, where and how to submit manuscripts, publication style requirements, abstracting and citation services that cover the journal, number of subscribers, and so on. Take, as an example, a listing (see Table 2.3) reprinted from one such resource with which I am familiar, *An Author's Guide to Social Work Journals* (Mendelsohn, 1992).

Each aspiring author should acquire those summary listings (books) that describe the salient characteristics of the journals relevant to his or her own field. These are invaluable references for your personal library. I have listed some of the major ones in the Appendix. Again, if the one relevant to your field is not listed, check with the reference librarian at your university.

Summary

A number of factors to be considered in choosing a journal to send your manuscript to have been reviewed in this chapter, and these are summarized in Table 2.4. These should not be viewed as hard-and-fast rules. For example, a more rigorous journal with a smaller number of subscribers and a higher rejection rate may be a better choice than one with a considerably larger number of subscribers.

Given all of the above, here is a simplified method of choosing a potential journal: Look in the reference list of the article you have written and see if one journal name keeps jumping out at you. If so, that is a likely first-choice outlet for obvious reasons. The journal seems to have published a fair amount of work related to your topic and editors are likely to be interested in additional submissions along those lines. Also, all things being equal, editors like to see their own journal's prior work suitably cited. There is no reason for the aspiring author not to take advantage of such subtle factors in choosing a journal.

Table 2.3 An Illustration of the Type of Information Found in Various Author's Guides to Journals for Different Disciplines

	Research on Social Work Practice
JOURNAL AFFILIATION	None
EDITORIAL FOCUS	The journal has a primary focus on the publication of empirically based outcome studies conducted in the area of social work practice, using either group or single-system research designs. Reports on the development and validation of new methods of assessment for use in social work practice are also welcome. The occasional scholarly review article and theoretical/conceptual piece that has clear and compelling applications (not simply implications) to social work practice are also published.
SPECIAL ISSUES	Can be arranged with the editor. Past special issues have focused on advances in practice research and on social work with groups.
WHERE INDEXED/ ABSTRACTED	*Current Contents: Social & Behavioral Sciences, Health and Psychosocial Instrument, Human Resources Abstracts, Linguistics and Language Behavior Abstracts, Psychological Abstracts, Psyc INFO, Social Planning/Policy & Development Abstracts, Social Sciences Citation Index, Social Work Research & Abstracts, Sociological Abstracts*
CIRCULATION	600
FREQUENCY OF PUBLICATION	Quarterly
NUMBER OF ARTICLES PUBLISHED	6-8
SUBMISSION OF MANUSCRIPT	
To whom	Bruce A. Thyer, Editor
Address	Research on Social Work Practice School of Social Work University of Georgia Athens, GA 30602
COPIES NEEDED FOR SUBMISSION	5
DISK SUBMISSION	Required after article is accepted for publication; 3½ in. disk and latest version of WordPerfect

FORMAT OF MANUSCRIPT

Cover Sheet Data	Consult style guide.
Abstract	100-150 words
Length	No limit
Size of Pages	8½ × 11 in.
Margins	Consult style guide.
Spacing	Double-spaced

STYLE GUIDE

Name of Guide	*Publication Manual of the American Psychological Association*
Subheadings	Consult style guide.
References	Consult style guide.
Footnotes	No footnotes
Tables and Figures	Consult style guide.

REVIEW PROCESS

Type of Review	Anonymous peer review by 3-5 reviewers
Acknowledgment	Editor sends letter on manuscript receipt
Review Time	An initial editorial decision is sent to the author within 3 months or less
Revisions	Arranged between author and editor
Acceptance Rate	Approximately 50%
Return of Manuscript	Rejected manuscripts are discarded
Lag Time to Print	8-12 months

CHARGES TO AUTHOR

Page Charges	No charges
Author Alterations	No charges

REPRINT POLICY	Authors receive 25 free reprints and 2 copies of the issue in which their article appears. Ordering information is sent on publication.
BOOK REVIEWS	Send unsolicited book reviews to the editor
SUBSCRIPTIONS	Ordered from: Sage Publications, Inc. Journal Subscription Department P.O. Box 5084 Thousand Oaks, CA 91359 $35.10/individuals $76.50/institutions, libraries

SOURCE: H. N. Mendelsohn (Ed.). (1992). *An author's guide to social work journals* (pp. 240-242). Washington, DC: NASW Press. Copyright © 1992, National Association of Social Workers, Inc. Reprinted with permission.

Table 2.4 Considerations in Selecting a Journal

1. Is the journal's subject matter, methodological preferences, theoretical orientation appropriate?
2. Does the journal employ blind peer-reviewing practices?
3. Does it levy a submission fee, page charges, or reprint charges?
4. Is the journal covered by the abstracting services relevant to your discipline?
5. Is the journal covered by the citation indices relevant to your discipline?
6. Do articles appearing in the journal get cited much?
7. Does the journal have a credible rejection rate?
8. Does the journal process manuscripts in a reasonable amount of time?
9. Are there a large number of subscribers?
10. Does the journal permit concurrent submissions?
11. Is there a long time lag from acceptance to publication?
12. Do you have any "inside information" about the journal that bears on your decision to submit an article to it?

3 | Preparing and Submitting the Manuscript

A handful of patience is worth more than a bushel of brains.
                                                    —Dutch proverb

What is one of the most important factors by which review-ers immediately judge the quality of a manuscript submitted for possible publication in a scholarly journal? Take a guess:

a. the high quality of the abstract,
b. the novel treatment of the subject,
c. good writing—clarity and style, or
d. seminal piece of work/research?

The correct answer is e—none of the above. According to data gathered by Keith Noble (cited in Holt, 1988), who surveyed 23 international and national education journal editors on the characteristics of manuscripts that have im-mediate appeal,

> editors noted more frequently *the professional appearance of a manu-script* than if it qualified as a seminal piece of work or research . . . . editors were more likely to reject an article *if the author guidelines were not followed* than if the statistics, tables or figures were poor . . . reviewers are more interested in qualities such as "clarity/coherence/well-written," "thoroughness," "research method," and "appropriateness to journal" than "a unique con-tribution," and "advancement of knowledge," and "the impor-tance of the subject." (Holt, 1988, p. 6, emphases added)

Leaving aside the discouraging sound of these observations, and the possible nonrepresentativeness of educational
periodicals relative to the corpus of scholarly journals, you
can see that proper preparation of a journal manuscript can
make or break a given piece of work. Fortunately, there are
a number of guidelines available to help you in this process.

Locate and Become Familiar
With Authors' Guidelines

Most journals provide some form of authors' guidelines
that you can consult to facilitate the proper preparation of
your manuscript. As a first step, locate the journal's copyright page, often found inside the front cover or on the first
left-hand page, which provides some instructions on the
preparation of manuscripts. See the sample shown in Figure
2.1, taken from my own journal, in the previous chapter.

You will notice that the publication style used by the
journal is mentioned, in this case we use the *Publication
Manual of the American Psychological Association* (American
Psychological Association [APA], 1983). Generally speaking,
various disciplines and professions fairly consistently follow one selected publication style. Medical journals usually
follow the "Vancouver style," also called the "Uniform Requirements"; law journals usually use the "Harvard Blue
Book style"; and so forth. Scholars should locate and become
familiar with the style relevant to their discipline and prepare
manuscripts accordingly. Space does not permit a precise detailing of all the minutiae relevant to the major publication
styles. A selected listing of resources detailing various styles
can be found in the appendix.

Preparing the Manuscript

Obviously the manuscript is prepared according to the
style guide for the journal you are sending it to. It can be

helpful to have a party unfamiliar with your work review the manuscript. Even a layperson can be of great assistance in giving feedback about clarity, spelling, and organization. For most journals, the manuscript can be organized in something like the following way:

Title Page
Abstract Page
Text
Reference List
Table
Figure Caption Page
Figures

For some types of scholarship, the text can be subdivided into the following:

Methods and Procedures
    Clients (subjects, participants, and so on)
    Research Design
    Intervention (independent variable, treatment, and so on)
    Outcome Measures (dependent variables and so on)
Results
Discussion
Biographical Note(s) (optional)

Of course, this will vary according to the type of scholarship being submitted. Literary articles are formatted differently than ones in experimental medicine. Review articles have a different organization than methodological works, and so on. The details of organizing each of these sections of a manuscript will vary from discipline to discipline, and across the various publication styles. Some excellent guidelines can be found in Day (1988), Beebe (1993), and the APA (1983). Your work should be printed on a laser printer, if possible, but in any event must be clean and legible.

A sample title page prepared in APA style appears in Figure 3.1. Note the placement of a descriptive header on the upper-right-hand corner, with the page number located below it (all flush right). The title appears below, followed by the author and institution, any authors' notes (acknowledgments and corresponding address), and a few key words. Provide middle initials to help distinguish your works from those of other "John Smiths" that appear in citation indices. The key words will be used to register your article in various citation indices. Using vague or inaccurate ones will result in fewer people accessing your work in the future when they conduct computerized literature searches.

Journal article titles should be succinct and interesting and convey what the article is about. Use abbreviations sparingly, if at all, and avoid filler phrases (e.g., "A study of . . . "). Some recommend avoiding the use of colons in titles, but this is a matter of individual taste. Scholars examining the literature (scanning tables of contents of journals, reading abstracting periodicals, reviewing citation indices) will use your title to help them decide to read (and possibly cite!) your work, hence the importance of a suitable title. I sometimes phrase a title in the form of a question, as in Figure 3.1, but this is again a matter of individual taste and journal style. Avoid titles subject to awkward interpretations, such as these provided by Day (1988, p. 17):

"Preliminary Canine and Clinical Evaluation of a New Antitumor Agent, Streptovitacin" (Did the dog evaluate the drug?) or

"Multiple Infections Among Newborns Resulting From Implantation With *Staphylococcus Aureus* 502A" (Were the newborns conceived via bacterial injection?)

Careful thought should be given to the preparation of the abstract, as it too will be used to help scholars decide whether or not to read your work. The journal guidelines may indicate a maximum word length (100-150 words is common), and an abstract's format may differ with the type of article (e.g., em-

---

Two-Year Program
1

Are Regular and Advanced Standing
MSW Students Equally Prepared for Clinical Practice?

Bruce A. Thyer
University of Georgia

Key Words: Advanced Standing, MSW Education

Author's Notes:
Correspondence may be addressed to B. A. Thyer, School of Social Work, University of Georgia, Athens, GA 30602. Kim E. Boynton provided helpful criticism of an earlier draft of this manuscript. This research was supported by a research grant (#AS92-143) from the Council on Social Work Education.

Figure 3.1. Sample Title Page for a Journal Manuscript

pirical research, review article, theoretical work). Individual journals may have their own conventions. The *American Journal of Psychiatry*, for example, requires abstracts of experimental outcome studies to use the underlined subheadings—<u>Objectives</u>, <u>Method</u>, <u>Results</u>, and <u>Conclusions</u>—a practice that I find very helpful.

The text should have certain characteristics, usually those associated with appropriate composition in English. Each paragraph should have a topic sentence and be composed of more than one sentence. Break up lengthy sentences into smaller ones and avoid Germanic constructions (Winston Churchill once noted on the margins of a memo prepared by his staff, "This is the type of language up with which I will not put."). Most journals require articles to be formatted in the third person, although this practice may vary by discipline.

Easy to understand words are preferable to those less so. Technical language is of course necessary, but jargon is not. If your own grammatical skills are weak, a proofreader (graduate student, colleague, spouse?) can be invaluable, as can the grammar checkers available on computers. For example, the word *data* is plural (use "These data indicate . . . " in lieu of "The data indicate . . . "). The possible points to be covered here are almost endless. The essential thing is to get your work down on paper as best you can and work from these initial drafts. *Do not* expect the first draft of your manuscript to be perfect.

Tables should be used only to present data that are too lengthy to be conveyed in a narrative format. If a table only has a few data points in it (my own minimum standard is six), then consider presenting these data in the text and omitting the table. Each of the guidebooks noted earlier (APA, 1983; Beebe, 1993; Day, 1988) has some fine guidelines on the preparation of tables to be included in journal articles. Although some word-processing systems possess a feature to use to format tables, these are usually not in conformity with the style guidelines used by journals. Tables should thus be formatted manually along the lines indicated by your targeted journal. For example, the WordPerfect feature for making tables sets them up with vertical lines forming columns as well as horizontal lines making rows. Given that APA style does not use vertical lines in constructing tables, this feature is not suitable for constructing tables for journals that use the APA style.

You should use the same typeface and characters per inch in setting up your tables as you use in the text. Continue your table on to second, third, or even more pages if need be rather than using a minuscule type size. Tables should *not be* embedded in the text but should appear after the list of references. Put only one table on each page. Because of their added cost in typesetting, tables should only be used when needed to convey information that does not lend itself to textual description.

The preparation of figures is even more of an art form than constructing tables. The visual depiction of quantitative information using figures can be used more effectively than either text or tables to convey relationships among variables. In addition to the style manuals and books cited above, Tufte (1983) and Mattaini (1993) are two terrific books detailing the principles of constructing functional figures. Nowadays there is little place for hand-drafted figures.

Use a computer and laser printer in conjunction with a good graphics program or a professional illustrator. Most university communities and larger towns have students or other graphics experts who can help you. It is often much more functional to *hire* some expert person to prepare your figures for you than to try to master a computer-based graphics program yourself. Provide them with a hand-drawn draft of your figure and any guidelines for the preparation for figures as provided by your target journal. Make sure your work is saved on a disk, which will facilitate future revisions (which may be likely), and keep a copy for yourself (in case the artist goes out of business, moves, or the like).

Most journals are not equipped to produce figures in color, so have them prepared in black and white (avoid using fine screens or shades of gray, which may become blotchy in the printing process). Some journal publishers can reproduce figures for publishing using black-and-white illustrations on regular paper. Others may require black-and-white glossy prints (i.e., a photograph) of your figure in order to reproduce it for printing in the journal. You will be told what is needed, and you should proceed accordingly.

You, not the publisher, are expected to foot the cost for glossy prints. Your nearby university should have facilities to prepare glossy prints from your clean and clear black-and-white illustrations. If you go to a commercial photography studio, make sure they use black-and-white photographic paper, not color paper, to produce your prints. If the latter is used, the background will likely be some shade of gray rather than the necessary white.

Figures you provide the publisher (often 8 × 10 in.) will likely be reduced into a size that fits into the journal's page dimensions. Make sure that your data points, lines, words, numbers, and symbols will remain legible when so reduced. Captions for your figure(s) usually are placed on a separate page in the manuscript, following the tables, if any, and before the pages containing the figures. Place only one figure on each page. All figure captions can be placed on one page. Print, using pencil, your name and the figure number on the back of each figure, in case they get shuffled. Each manuscript page devoted to a table or to figure captions has the header and page number printed on it, located in the upper-right-hand corner, but figures themselves do not have a header or page number on them. Include tables, figures, and figure caption pages in calculating the page length of your manuscript, which is important if you are working with a journal-imposed page limitation.

Submitting the Manuscript

Photocopy the required number of copies, and staple each set together in the upper-right-hand corner. It is not usually necessary to submit original manuscripts. Today's high quality photocopying technology and laser printers obviate the need to send in "originals." Send a brief letter to the editor requesting review. The sample submission letter found in Figure 3.2 can serve as a guide.

Bundle up the required number of copies, top them off with your letter of submission and any needed copies of letters of permission (do not send your original letters, for obvious protection against loss, and so on), and mail it off first class mail. Do not go to the expense of sending it overnight mail. It will not result in any reduction in publication lag time and will make you look overly anxious and wasteful of money.

[Use institutional letterhead, if possible]

Date

Bruce A. Thyer, Editor
Research on Social Work Practice
School of Social Work
University of Georgia
Athens, Georgia 30605

Re: "Does Food Stamp Program Participation Improve the Nutritional
Status of Welfare Recipients?"

Dear Dr. Thyer:

Enclosed please find five copies of the above manuscript that we are
submitting for editorial review and possible publication in *Research on
Social Work Practice*. This article represents original and previously unpublished scholarship that is not under concurrent editorial review. I enclose
a letter from the publisher of the *Journal of Nutrition* granting permission
for us to use the material found in our Table 1.

We look forward to hearing from you.

Sincerely,

Lois A. Wodarski, Ph.D.
Professor of Nutrition
University of Hamburgh

cc: Ronald MacDonald

Figure 3.2. Sample Letter of Submission

You may find the checklist for authors in Table 3.1 of use in
making sure you have covered all the bases when mailing
off your work. Sometimes journal editors can provide you
with such a checklist idiosyncratic to their journal. Feel free
to request these of editors, and follow such guidelines
exactly.

Table 3.1 Sample Manuscript Checklist

— Make sure *everything* is double-spaced. This includes all references, endnotes or footnotes, the title page, all quotes, tables, appendixes, and so on. *Nothing* is to be single- or triple-spaced.

— The manuscript is not right justified (the right margin is ragged, not aligned).

— The manuscript begins with a title page, containing the article's title, all authors' names, addresses, and telephone/fax numbers/e-mail addresses, if available. This (and all succeeding pages) has a right-justified header and is noted as page 1.

— The second page contains an abstract of no more that 150 words and any author's notes. This page is headed Abstract (centered), with no title.

— The third page has the centered title at the top. Underneath the title, begin the text of the article.

— Do not use footnotes at the bottom of pages. Number notes and place them on a separate page(s) at the end of the text and before the references.

— Make sure that all citations mentioned in the text are fully referenced in the reference list and that all citations in the reference list are mentioned in the text. This section begins on a separate page following the end of the text and is headed References (centered). Headers and page numbers continue consecutively.

— Make sure all references are complete (with inclusive page numbers, for example) and are formatted according to the style used by the journal you are submitting to.

— Tables are placed on separate pages, double-spaced. Do not change typeface or font size. Follow style guidelines to format tables (e.g., the WordPerfect table format feature *does not* set up APA-style tables).

— Make sure that all figures are properly prepared. These go after the tables (if any) and are proceeded by a separate page containing figure captions. Only send original photographs or internegatives if the subject matter of your paper or the journal requires such a submission at this time. Otherwise, wait until your work has been accepted before sending these materials

— Submit required number of copies and a succinct letter requesting review. Include return postage if required. Copies should be very clean and clear.

— Include copies of letters granting permission to reproduce copyrighted materials, if needed.

What About Word Processing?

I have prepared journal manuscripts using a number of methods, beginning as a graduate student by writing in longhand and then manually typing them out. Nowadays I use a word processor (I have been happy with the Word-Perfect program) and prepare my manuscripts myself. I believe that there is a significant savings of time in doing this myself, in terms of initially drafting and revising the work, relative to having someone else prepare them for me.

Various commercially available word-processing systems exist that have been developed with particular publication style formats in mind. For example, Pergamon Press markets a system called *Manuscript Manager*, which formats articles in the APA publication style. A user-friendly program called *Reference Manager* (sold by Research Information Systems) establishes a database of references that can then be retrieved into a manuscript in the appropriate journal style. This is particularly handy when submitting a work prepared in one reference style to a journal that requires another style. The program will make all the necessary changes, reducing tediousness and the likehood of errors creeping in.

There is a class of software that can be generically called "grammar checkers." These programs are designed to operate in conjunction with WordPerfect or other word-processing systems and perform a variety of functions, some of which are quite sophisticated. They check spelling, grammar, and punctuation, count words, make sure that tenses agree and that certain common mistakes are guarded against (e.g., using *their* for *there*). The proper matching of subject and verb can be examined, and such things as the average number of words per sentence, or sentences per paragraph, calculated. An estimated reading difficulty level can be provided—a useful function for those of us who write too obscurely. Commercially available products cost in the range of $30-$40 (simply go to your local computer store and ask for grammar-checker programs), and various clone-type programs can be purchased as "shareware" for considerably less. Such software can be of particular value if writing is not your strong suit. The latest version (6.0) of WordPerfect contains a built-in grammar-checking feature.

Increasingly journals are requiring that the authors of *accepted* manuscripts submit their final version both in hard copy *and* formatted on a computer disk. They may specify a word-processing program (such as WordPerfect) or use a generic system. By preparing your manuscript on a word processor from the beginning, you will reduce subsequent delays in submitting it on disk. Another advantage is that, if asked to reduce (or lengthen) a manuscript when preparing a revision, conniving authors have been known to take a journal article formatted with a 10-character-per-inch (cpi) typeface (font) and change it to a 12-cpi font, perhaps "reducing" the length of a manuscript by several pages. Narrowing margins from 1.5 inches to 1 inch can achieve the same result. Sharp editors may note these ploys and ask you to go back and make the original cuts, which could delay publication of your article, but I blush to admit having successfully used both of these tactics on more than one occasion.

4 | Writing a Revision and Reviving a Rejection

Your manuscript is both good and original; but the part that is good is not original, and the part that is original is not good.

—Samuel Johnson

How to Handle Requests for Revisions

It is a hard fact of life that only very rarely are articles accepted as submitted. In almost all cases authors are expected to undertake certain revisions in their work in accord with the recommendations provided by the editor and/or reviewers. Do not take umbrage at this; rather, view it as an accepted part of the journal publication game. Now, you and I and any other impartial expert in your field know that the recommended changes you are being asked to make will actually detract from the seamless thread of your narrative flow, but in a sense your acceptance for publication is being held hostage contingent on your satisfactorily dealing with these requests for revisions. Here are some of your options.

The Practice of Pilate

You do have the option, of course, to write back to the editor and state in effect: "I am unwilling to make any changes in my article. Either publish it as it stands, or send it back to me." This course of action is not recommended. It was taken by Pontius Pilate, who proclaimed, "What I have

51

written, I have written" (John, 19:22), possibly to his eternal regret.

In most cases the requested revisions will actually improve the presentation of your work. Keep in mind that the staff editing professional journals do this for a living, day in and day out, processing hundreds of manuscripts per year. They often will have a greater sense of readability, narrative flow, phraseology, organization of the manuscript, and so forth than you do. Also, the editors and reviewers may have gone to considerable effort to provide you with constructive feedback, and to have it summarily dismissed by you doesn't engender warm feelings of editorial sympathy for the intrepid scholar standing up for what you believe to be the truth! In all probability the editor will return your work and you will have to begin the submission process all over again, with another journal, the attendant delays, and the likelihood of a similar outcome (i.e., being asked to revise your work). So, the general rule is to attempt to undertake any revisions requested.

The best (but all too rare!) editorial practice is for an editor to carefully read your manuscript, examine the reviewers' suggestions, and prepare a detailed cover letter that specifically states which changes the editor concurs with and those that are unnecessary for you to undertake. In such cases the revising process is relatively straightforward and the author is faced with little ambiguity.

What is far more common, however, is for the editor to send a letter requesting that the author comply with the revisions recommended by the reviewers, whose commentaries are enclosed. If and when a suitable revision has been received by the editor, a final decision will be made to accept or reject the manuscript at that time. The problem with this approach, from the perspective of the author, is that it is common for reviewers to provide conflicting recommendations or for one reviewer to suggest some massive changes but for the others not to mention similar revisions. What is the poor author to do?

Undertaking the Revision Process

Here is Thyer's approach to undertaking revisions. Lay out each of the reviewer's comments and label them (if they are not already labeled) as Reviewer A, Reviewer B, Reviewer C, and so on. Then, in the left-hand margin of each set of reviewer's commentary, denote each specific and substantive suggested revision as "Number 1," "Number 2," and so on. Now, examine Suggestion 1 from Reviewer A and decide how you want to address it. If the suggestion refers to grammar, spelling, punctuation, and so on, and the point is correct, make the indicated change. If the reviewer asks that you provide a further citation, or makes another point, and the issue raised is legitimate, go ahead and complete the change. (Remember, because your manuscript has been word-processed, making these revisions will be relatively easy.)

Of course, if the editor asks you only to make a very few changes, then the above procedure is a moot point. If the changes recommended by the reviewers are contradictory, particularly extensive, or too vague to enable you to proceed, it is a useful practice to call the editor and request clarification about which suggestions he or she wishes you to act on. Explain your dilemma in an honest manner without being hostile or argumentative. Emphasize that you are willing to make necessary changes, providing you are given the necessary guidance. Try to get those changes mandated by the *editor* clarified, restate them to him or her over the phone to be sure you understand what is expected of you, and refer to this conversation and your mutually agreed on understanding in the cover letter accompanying the revision.

Move Quickly!

A few journals provide you with a deadline within which you are to submit any requested revisions. This is good, as many of us are most productive when working under a deadline. In the absence of an explicit deadline, I still try to make it my practice to turn around editorial requests for revisions within 1 week. If this is not possible, I generally give priority to revising such manuscripts before undertaking work on other projects. You see, if an author makes a genuine effort to comply with most of the significant requests for revisions made by an editor, it is very likely that *the manuscript will be accepted for publication!* There is almost an implicit understanding that, if an editor asks you to make changes A, B, and C in your manuscript, after which she will be pleased to reconsider it, if you the author indeed do A, B, and C, and resubmit the work, then the editor is obliged to accept the manuscript. This is only fair and just, because you have done precisely what the editor requested. It is *not* fair and just, after receiving your revision that was prepared along the lines specified by the editor, for the editor then to raise another set of objections or recommended changes for you to comply with prior to acceptance. In such a case, move to the option below.

Kvetch!

> *I do not at all resent criticism, even when, for the sake of emphasis, it parts company with reality.*
> Winston S. Churchill, 1941

Winston Churchill's exemplary standard of patience is unlikely to be maintained by the anxious authors of scholarly articles that have been reviewed by a journal. It is not unheard of for reviewers to do a shoddy job; to make mistakes; for editors to misread commentary and make an erroneous decision; to send you the wrong manuscript; or to mix up manuscripts, editorial comments, and editorial letters so that you receive materials meant for someone else. If such an untoward event should happen to you, do not get angry and fire off a heated response to the incompetent editor. Keep in mind Giroux's (1982) observation that most editors are merely failed writers. Or perhaps an editorial assistant is responsible for a mixup. In either case, prepare a temperate letter, explain your complaint, and request (not demand) reconsideration of the points being demanded of you.

For example, if a reviewer insists that you use a different statistical approach to analyze your data, one that you are confident is incorrect, explain your reasons and document them. If the reviewer says that you should cite the earlier work of so-and-so, and you *already did this* (i.e., the reviewer did not give your work a careful reading), bring this to the attention of the editor as well.

For all those points with which you disagree, note them in the cover letter accompanying your revised manuscript and succinctly state your reasons for not complying with such-and-such a suggestion. No doubt such reactions will be accompanied by numerous examples of where *you did comply*, thus indicating your willingness to be reasonable in attempting a revision. Cover letters can be several single-spaced pages in length, if need be, providing the pretense, if not the actuality, that you devoted a considerable amount of time and effort to preparing your revision. Most editors do not insist that you comply with everything the reviewers state but that you do give careful consideration to their points and have a plausible rationale for not doing what they suggest. If this is well documented or otherwise supported, such a response on your part should not jeopardize the chances that your manuscript will be accepted.

What to Do
With a Rejected Manuscript?

To attempt to publish articles in scholarly journals is by definition to subject yourself to the experience of receiving letters of rejection. Both novice and experienced academics and practitioners find their works to be rejected on a regular basis, which is not a surprise because some journals have a greater than 90% rejection rate. This is not a cause for shame or regret. Rather, your attitude should be to learn from the experience and to attempt to revive the paper by resubmitting it to another journal if your honest appraisal indicates that this course is indicated.

Evaluate the Reviewers' and Editor's Commentaries

Most good journals go beyond sending you a simple letter of rejection. Along with a rejection letter you should receive written commentaries provided by the blind reviewers that outline their reasons for recommending that your work should not be published. In the best of all possible worlds, this commentary will consist of unbiased evaluations provided by competent scholars with particular expertise in the subject matter of your paper. It is to be expected that these folks will have read your paper carefully and made note of its strengths and limitations. Their reasons for rejection will be detailed and specific. They may also be maddeningly ignorant, shortsighted, and simply incorrect, but there is little you can do about this. If such is the case, however, consider the following option.

Appeal to the Editor

If the grounds for rejection appear to be incorrect assumptions on the part of the reviewers, or erroneous information, it is reasonable to write the editor back and succinctly state your grounds for requesting that she reconsider her decision to reject your article. Take, for example, the following: The reviewer stated that the data you reported and analyzed using inferential tests did not meet the assumptions that the statistical tests were based on. You have carefully reexamined the data and are assured that the data had been appropriately analyzed, perhaps buttressing your claim with some citations to the statistical literature and/or by sending along a supportive letter from a colleague in your university's Department of Statistics. These may be sufficient grounds to request such a reconsideration.

This happened to me recently when I submitted an article reporting on changes in death rates in Georgia following the implementation of a mandatory safety belt use law in our state. One of the reviewers claimed that my data were inappropriately analyzed because they violated the assumptions that a t test is based on. I reexamined my data, documented that they did not violate the assumptions noted by the reviewer, and resubmitted it to the editor. It was subsequently accepted. The lesson here is that reviewers too are fallible human beings. They are not godlike creatures from Olympus making irrevocable pronouncements sealing the fate of your work. They are most likely harried academics short of time and patience who give your work a too-cursory analysis. Mistakes can happen. If they do, bring them to the editor's attention with a request for reconsideration.

Do not be shy about this, if you have clearly been the victim of erroneous information. On the other hand, mere differences of opinion between you and the reviewer that lack the capacity for any concrete resolution do not lend themselves to appeal in this manner. To badger the editor on insubstantial issues is not likely to produce a reconsidered letter of acceptance and may well yield a harvest of ill will that could come to haunt you when you submit manuscripts to this editor in the future.

Submit to Another Journal, *Immediately!*

Suppose, on the other hand, that your considered appraisal of the reviewer's suggestions and comments does not turn up any grounds for an appeal. Rather, it seems that the reviewers made a good judgment call in rejecting your paper. They discovered some substantial grounds for rejection, perhaps methodological, which you may or may not have been aware of, but in any event these issues are nothing you can do anything about. Is the case hopeless? Of course not.

You have several things going for you. Given today's rejection rates, keep in mind that most articles you read in scholarly journals *have been rejected* once, twice, or even more times before being accepted so that you can eventually read them in print. If these rejected works can eventually make it into print, it is certainly possible that yours can as well. Another point in your favor is the unreliability inherent in the journal review process and in arriving at editorial decisions (MacReynolds, 1971). Recall Peters and Ceci's (1982) study wherein recently published articles were retyped with fictitious names and affiliations, but otherwise left unchanged, in which they found that a lot of these works were subsequently rejected for publication, often on serious methodological grounds, by the very journals that had published them a year or two earlier. Although such a study as the following one has not been done, I am quite sure that, if articles *rejected* by Journal X were retyped with slightly changed information about the author and title and resubmitted a few months later to the editor of Journal X, a certain proportion of them would be *accepted* virtually unchanged. This phenomenon could be attributed to such factors as the luck of the draw when reviewers are selected, the editorial frame of mind when the editor makes a decision about your manuscript, the journal's backlog of accepted articles—in fact, a host of variables that make the journal publication system, in part, a probabilistic process (Stinchcombe & Ofshe, 1969).

No, obviously it is not appropriate to resubmit a thinly disguised reissue of your article to the same journal. But if your manuscript is rejected on the basis of insubstantial reasons, this cold hard fact can work to your advantage. The chances are excellent that another journal will react more favorably to your article. Now, I do not wish to be accused of the gambler's fallacy; your article's past history of rejection has no bearing on enhancing its likelihood of acceptance in the future. But, by quickly turning your work around and getting it in the mail to another journal, you maximize the chances of it being accepted, relative to letting it decompose in your file drawer, on the back burner of your personal list of publication priorities. In fact, this is one of the great secrets of successful publishing in scholarly journals: Try to submit rejected manuscripts to another journal the *very day you get the letter of rejection!* The response cost is low, merely producing another letter of submission that has a couple of paragraphs, making 3 to 5 more clean copies of the article, stuffing them into an envelope, addressing and mailing it. Poof! It is back being reviewed with hardly a delay. Who knows, this time it might get accepted! This course of action is only recommended for those articles that are rejected for no convincing reason and the reviewers' comments are not provided or are less than compelling. I cannot emphasize enough the importance of this tactic. Too many of my colleagues react to an initial rejection from their top-choice journal by psychologically withdrawing from further involvement in attempting to get the manuscripts published. This is a big mistake, and one you can avoid.

Prepare for it by being aware that most articles are rejected before being published and by having a listing made up in advance of alternative journals to send your work to if it is not accepted by the initial journal you sent it to. If need be, rather than let it molder in the file drawer, give it to a doctoral student or a colleague with the assignment of revising it as seems suitable and to undertake its publication on your behalf (in return for suitable credit, of course). Through this course of action, many otherwise wasted manuscripts eventually can be published, even without further involvement on your part. Obviously, however, the best action is to resubmit it promptly yourself. If it was rejected for credible reasons, however, consider the following option.

Revise and Submit the Manuscript Elsewhere

If your appraisal of the reviewers' remarks and editorial commentary turns up some useful point, then by all means take the time to revise the manuscript accordingly and resubmit it to your second-choice journal. This is, after all, one of the supposed virtues of the peer-review system used by most of our academic and practice journals—to provide you with constructive criticism that can be used to improve the quality of what is eventually published in your discipline.

The same principle of timeliness applies, however. One's emotional involvement in a writing project seems to decline with the passage of time and one's continued inaction. When you get a rejection with useful comments, revise the manuscript as quickly as possible and get it back in the mail. In fact, such projects should be given a high priority among your other duties. If all else fails, consider recruiting a helpful colleague or doctoral student to do this for you.

Similar guidelines for revising should be followed. Make use of constructive remarks and new information that you can incorporate into your revised article. Ignore unprofessional comments or personal observations ("It is obvious that this author did not know what he was doing . . . "). Irremediable methodological shortcomings and/or rival explanations for your findings should be acknowledged and briefly discussed in the discussion section.

How to Submit to Another Journal. When resubmitting a rejected manuscript to another journal, pretend that it is the very first time it has been sent anywhere. The editor of Journal B is unlikely to know of its rejection by Journal A and when you send it to the editor of Journal B there is no reason to let her know of the manuscript's prior history of rejection (e.g., "I really hope you can accept my article. This is the sixth journal I have sent it to . . . "). As always, keep your letters brief and to the point. Convey necessary information and not much else, just as in the first time you submitted it to Journal A. If you wish to deal with other matters (personal relationships, observations about your discipline, your views on the quality of the journal and of the job the editor is doing in managing the journal), make these the subject of a separate letter mailed independently of your manuscript.

Recycle It

At some point it may become obvious that your article is either unworthy of being published or, despite it value, very unlikely to be accepted in a scholarly journal when submitted via the regular peer-review processes. You do have several options remaining in such cases. In the first, you can attempt to get the article published in a special issue of a journal that you are guest editing (see Chapter 7). Because you are the gatekeeper in arranging such special issues, in some cases it *may* be both possible and professionally appropriate to include your work in the special issue. A second option is to attempt to publish the work in the form of a book chapter. No doubt as an active academic or practitioner in your field, you are concurrently pursuing a number of publishing venues at the same time. It is possible for you to attempt to edit or write a professional book in which you could include your orphan article as a book chapter. Alternatively, you could write to persons who are active in producing books for your field and suggest that they consider including your manuscript as a chapter in a future book they may be preparing. You have little to lose by pursuing these latter options, and they should be contemplated prior to giving up. This brings us to our last option.

Dump It

If you have made a good faith effort to get your work published in a scholarly journal, all to no avail, and other options such as offering it to a colleague to revise and take over publication efforts or trying to get it published as a book chapter have failed, *and* an objective appraisal of your work, now that you have reflected on it for a year or two while trying to get it published, has led you to the more considered judgment that you really do not think it should be published, then dump it. Cut your losses, intellectual and psychological, and pitch the whole thing.

Consider the fate of certain authors who, while alive, declined to publish certain short stories or books because of their poor quality, only to have these relics exhumed decades after the death of the writer, to appear in minor literary journals or as part of a new and expanded edition of "The Collected Works of George Blahah." All those things that poor Blahah, while alive, decided were not worthy of publication are now revealed to the public's critical eye, perhaps to the detriment of Blahah's literary reputation, and certainly against his wishes. If you leave unpublished manuscripts around, some ambitious scholar in the future may uncover them and expose the worst of your work to all the world. This can be avoided by every so often purging your hard-copy files and deleting unwanted material from your hard drives and floppy disks.

Summary

Always keep your manuscripts in circulation until they are published. That is a vital practice. If you have a credible piece of scholarship, it will eventually find a home in a suitable journal, *if you persevere!* It may not be in the top ranked journal in your field, but in most disciplines, publication in journals rated second is infinitely better than no publication at all. If it turns out that the work is really not worthy of publication, dump it and move on to better projects.

5 | What to Do After Your Manuscript Has Been Accepted

I was working on the proof of one of my poems all morning, and took out a comma. In the afternoon I put it back again.
—Oscar Wilde

Now that you have received that coveted letter of acceptance from an editor of a scholarly journal, what is expected of you? First, it is always a good idea to send your program chair or dean a short note informing her when you have had an article accepted for publication is a scholarly journal. Provide the complete citation, including the journal's title. If your chair is a shrewd motivator, she will announce your latest evidence of academic excellence during a forthcoming faculty meeting! There do remain some additional tasks for you, however, and here is a description of the major activities/milestones in continuing your journey into print.

Dealing With Editors

Most journals operate according to a strict schedule of deadlines. Editors of journals typically have an absolute bottom-line date by which all the manuscripts to go into a particular issue *must* be at the publishers, that is, manuscripts with accompanying signed authors' agreements, figures suitable for reproduction in a journal, signed permissions to reprint previously published material, names and mailing addresses of all authors, and other minutiae. This means, according to the principle that big fleas have little fleas, that the editor expects *you* to adhere to any necessary deadlines.

First, make a practice of responding to letters from editors, including the one accepting your article, very quickly, the same day if possible. Do not go to the bother of overnight mail unless that is required because of publication deadlines. Fax transmissions are usually not necessary either. But do send a letter of acknowledgment, and it is a wise and tactful policy to say something about how pleased you are that your work will be appearing in this editor's prestigious journal. Imagine that you are writing to Miss Manners when you deal with editorial correspondence. Always be exceedingly polite. There is no room for abrasiveness when dealing with such important matters as getting your scholarship expeditiously published. Also, keep your letters short and to the point. Lengthy homilies about how glad you are to have finally found a home for your article, after it had been rejected by six other journals, and invectives about the incompetence of those other editors, are an unsound policy. In all future dealings by mail, be similarly prompt, polite, and professional.

Returning the Completed Author's Agreement

Usually, but not in all cases, when you receive a letter of acceptance from a journal editor, it is accompanied by an author's agreement, a legal document between you (the author or authors) and the publisher (a proprietary company, a university press, and so on) wherein you declare certain conditions to be true of your work (it is your own intellectual property, it has not been previously published, it contains no previously copyrighted material, and so on). A sample author's agreement, typical of the breed, is depicted in Figure 5.1. In almost all cases you can sign off on these without reservations or consulting an attorney (in addition, if you do not, you cannot get your article published!). In most cases you will be able to reproduce your article, in whole or in part, in your future scholarly publications without payment of a fee, although this varies among publishing houses. You should, of course, carefully read the contract to understand the rights and obligations both you and the publisher assume. In most cases it is not practical to propose amending these authors' agreements inasmuch as they are fairly standard and long-standing arrangements that have been worked out between scholars and publishers.

Some publishers allow you to have one of the authors sign off on behalf of the others, in the case of multiauthored works, while others, more conservative, require you to obtain the authentic, original signature of each author. If she lives down the hall from you, this is no problem. If she is away on a paleontology expedition on an obscure island off Costa Rica, obtaining the necessary signature can be a problem. The publisher will tell you that the original signatures are an absolute must, that they are required to be on file before the article can appear in print (and most likely before typesetting is begun). Hence off you go to Costa Rica or send overnight mail service down there in your stead. If the coauthor has died, the publisher will require a signature from the executor of her estate.

It is legally wrong to forge a coauthor's signature, even with her consent and if production deadlines exert pressure on you. Given the time lags between acceptance and production, however, it is almost always possible to obtain required signatures within the time frames established by a publisher. Keep a copy of this signed author's agreement for your files, as you do for all editorial correspondence. Sometimes the publisher's agent will have signed it before you do; sometimes you will be asked to sign it first, return the signed copies, and they will then sign off and return the completely executed document to you. As a matter of protocol, once you have a letter from the editor accepting your article for publication, the publisher is morally, if not legally, bound to publish your work.

AGREEMENT made   , between
Sage Publications, Inc., 2455 Teller Road, Thousand Oaks, California 91320
USA (hereinafter called the Publisher), and

residing at

(hereinafter called the Author) with respect to a work provisionally entitled

(hereinafter called the Work), and consisting of

RIGHTS: So that the Publisher may cause the Work to be published in
RESEARCH ON SOCIAL WORK PRACTICE the Author grants and assigns to the Publisher during the term of copyright and all renewals and
extensions thereof the exclusive right to publish and market the Work
throughout the world; to cause or license the Work to be translated into any
and all languages for publication and sale throughout the world; to publish
or license publication of the Work in reprint form, in anthologies, in periodicals, in digests, abridgments, condensations, abstracts, microfilms, recordings, Braille, photographing, or in any other present and future media, and
in all forms of merchandising and commercial use; to copyright the Work in
the name of the Publisher.

AUTHOR'S COPIES: The Publisher agrees to present a singular Author
with 25 copies of the Work and one or two copies of the issue of the original
publication in which it appears (if more than one Author, 25 copies of the
Work shall be divided between them, and each Author shall receive one copy
of the issue). The Author shall be able to purchase reprints of the Work at the
Publisher's regularly scheduled prices. The Publisher shall be under no
obligation to further compensate the Author for the rights granted herein,
but shall be obligated to give full credit of authorship regardless of means
and form of reproduction and publication.

PUBLICATION: The Publisher may make the manuscript conform to a style
of presentation, spelling, capitalization, and usage deemed appropriate. The
author shall read and correct the edited manuscript and proofs when and if
submitted, and return promptly corrected manuscript or proofs to the Publisher. The Publisher may charge the Author for expenses incurred as a result
of excessive changes in proofs.

WARRANTIES: (a) The Author warrants and represents that he/she is the
sole owner of the Work and all the rights herein granted and has full right

Figure 5.1. Sample Author's Publication Agreement/Copyright
Form

and power to make this agreement; that the Work is not a violation of any copyright, proprietary or personal right; that he/she has not in any manner granted, assigned, encumbered, or disposed of any of the rights herein granted to the Publisher or any rights adverse to or inconsistent therewith; and that there are no rights outstanding which would diminish, encumber, or impair the full enjoyment or exercise of the rights herein granted the Publisher; that no part of the Work is libelous, obscene, or unlawful or violates any right of privacy.

(b) The Author agrees to hold harmless and indemnify the Publisher against any claim, demand, suit, action, proceeding, recovery, or expense of any nature whatsoever arising from any claim of infringement of copyright or proprietary right, or from claims of libel, obscenity, unlawfulness, or invasion of privacy based upon or arising out of any matter or thing contained in the Work, or from any breach of warranties or representation herein contained. In addition to other remedies, the Publisher may withhold as offset royalties due the Author. The Publisher may at its sole discretion and expense retain counsel and may at its sole discretion compromise any such claim or suit brought against it.

(c) The warranties, representations, and indemnities shall survive the termination of this Agreement.

SPECIAL PROVISIONS: The Author reserves the right to use all or part of the Work in any book or article he/she may subsequently write or edit.

COPYRIGHT: The Publisher shall copyright the Work as part of RESEARCH ON SOCIAL WORK PRACTICE in the name of the Publisher.

This Agreement shall bind and inure to the benefit of the heirs, executors, administrators, and legal representatives of the Author, and upon the successors and assigns of the Publisher. However, all obligations of the Author are personal and non-assignable. This Agreement constitutes the complete understanding of the parties and shall be interpreted according to the laws of the State of California, regardless of the place of its execution. No modification or waiver of any provision hereof shall be valid unless in writing and signed by both parties.

_____	RESEARCH ON SOCIAL WORK PRACTICE
_____ by _____ (Editor)	

Figure 5.1. Continued

Now that you have acknowledged the acceptance of your article with a courteous but brief letter, and returned the signed author's agreement properly completed, comes perhaps the most difficult aspect of publishing a journal article: patiently waiting for it to appear in print! Try not to call or write the journal editor every month or so, asking for the status of your manuscript. This will not earn you any points and may help you acquire the reputation of a pain in the backside, something to be avoided as you will possibly be sending this editor additional articles at some point in the future.

Competent editors will give you an approximate date or issue of the journal that is projected to contain your article. This is more likely to be an optimistic appraisal than a realistic one. Be prepared for one or more issues to appear in print, past the projected one, before your article comes out. Publication time lags vary greatly across disciplines and across journals within disciplines. Some of the very best periodicals may have your work out in a month or so after acceptance (e.g., *Science*, *Nature*). Others, not necessarily poorer quality ones, may take 1 to *several* years! Consultation with colleagues can inform you which journals in your field have the shortest time lag to publication.

There is little you can do to speed the appearance of your article in print. Hounding the editor is not likely to be of help, neither is calling the publisher's production department. Some editors may be sympathetic to your plight if you are coming up for tenure or a promotion decision and need a few more articles in print, but very few will be (or should be) sympathetic enough to bump your article up on the publication schedule.

I am aware of one journal in psychology that, on acceptance, tells the author that the journal is experiencing about a 4-year time lag between acceptance and publication. If the author will pay a (substantial) page charge, however, publication will be expedited and the article will appear within the next issue or two. This is not a highly regarded journal and such practices smack of extortion. I do not suggest reinforcing such behavior.

Preparing Camera-Ready Figures

If your article contains figures or photographs, you may be asked to prepare camera-ready copies of these materials, as discussed in Chapter 3. Journal publishers vary in the method of reproduction used to print illustrations. Some can work from a clean and clear black-and-white figure printed (professionally drawn or laser printed) on regular typing paper. Other publishers require that you submit your figures in the form of black-and-white photographs (called glossy prints). Your editor should provide you with instructions on the preparation of such figures, and the APA *Publication Manual* contains a chapter on their construction, if needed. The cost of such photos is again something you must absorb, unless your department subsidizes this expense for you or you can write it off onto a grant. Your university library or print shop will likely have skilled people to assist you along these lines, as will a medical school's medical illustration department. Again, promptly prepare and submit any required illustrations, adhering closely to the directions provided.

You have another task to perform before seeing your article published. That task is edit the page proofs. If you do not do this at all, or do a clumsy job, your article's publication could be *delayed*. Here is a description of this process.

Editing Proofs

After your manuscript has been accepted by a journal, it enters the publication pipeline. It is usually assigned a copy editor, who goes over it with a fine-tooth comb, checking, for example, that each citation appearing in the text is listed in the reference list, and vice versa, or that the dates of the text citation correspond with the date (year of publication) provided in the reference list citation. You may receive a call from an editorial staff member to reconcile some discrepancies. While a tedious business for you to have to deal with, such double-checking is absolutely essential to assuring that your work is as flaw-free as possible. Two possibilities are open at this point: The manuscript can be typeset or it can be sent to you for final checking. I will discuss these options in order.

The editorial staff person passes the vetted manuscript on to a typesetter, who may work from your word-processed diskette version (if you submitted one and it is in good shape) or may retype your manuscript by hand (beware, lots of errors can creep in at this stage). In either case, a desktop publishing system will produce what looks like a finished journal article, typeset using the typeface and format that appear in the journal, perhaps missing the page numbers of the issue it will appear in. These "page proofs" get another once over, and they are sent to you with proofing instructions and a deadline. Most often, you are asked to compare the page proofs with your own copy of the manuscript text and tables and to check for errors.

You are discouraged from making substantial changes to the manuscript at this point, as it is expensive to have revised material retypeset. In fact, the publisher's instructions may contain a statement to the effect that significant revisions will be charged to you! Make any small changes necessary, but now is not the time to engage in significant rewriting of your text, unless you have compelling professional reasons (e.g., you discovered an error in your data). A sample set of instructions that are sent to authors being asked to edit their page proofs appears in Figure 5.2. Follow these instructions to the letter, paying particular care to having the page proofs returned by the indicated deadline.

Over the centuries in the history of printing, a series of conventionally accepted typesetting notation has evolved, symbols indicating various courses of action to be undertaken on a manuscript. A sample set of proofing notation appears in Figure 5.3. A summary of this notation, as used by your journal, may be sent along with your page proofs, and you are asked to use these symbols in editing the proofs.

By all means do so but do not make a fetish out of it. If in doubt, spell out any changes you want rather than confusing the typesetter by using unfamiliar symbols.

Pay particular attention to the spelling of the authors' names and to the wording of the title of the article. You should make a minor fetish over consistently using a professional name to appear on all your publications. I use "Bruce A. Thyer" and try to avoid permutations such as B. Thyer, B. A. Thyer, Bruce Thyer, and so forth. This is to make sure that my work is properly and consistently listed in journal/author citation indices, a factor of particular importance for scholars going up for promotion or tenure. It is possible, for example, that as part of your promotion process someone will consult the citation indices relevant to your field to determine how many times other authors have cited you and your work over the past year, 5-year period, and so on. If you use a variety of professional names, you may not be properly credited with contributions you have worked so hard to have appear in print. If you are not the corresponding author for a journal article, make sure the person dealing with the journal publisher is aware of your preference regarding the spelling of your name and adheres to it.

Once given the third degree by you, these page proofs may be sent back to the publisher, or to the journal's editor, depending on the policy of that particular publisher. The edited page proofs are examined again by an editorial staff member and passed on to a typesetter. Any changes you indicate are usually made without demure. Eventually, the thing is completed and saved in the memory banks of the publisher's master computer, awaiting the publication of the issue your article will appear in.

A variation on this approach, a cheaper and less desirable option in my opinion, is for a copy editor to carefully go over your manuscript and to return it to you, full of printer's notations, deleted words, transposed phrases, and the like, and then you are asked to check over this mutilated thing that was once your pristine manuscript. Assuming that all is

---

Date _____

Journal _____

PAGE PROOFS ENCLOSED

Author: Your deadline is _____

Return your proofs to the journal's editor at:

DEADLINES

The above deadline is real. Corrections arriving after this deadline may be too late to incorporate into your article. If you cannot meet the deadline by Express Mail or courier service, you may FAX correction pages to us (use the finest setting on your FAX machine). Please send to the attention of *JOURNALS* and *LIST THE NAME OF THE JOURNAL.*

About These Proofs

Please review these proofs carefully. Many hands have touched your original manuscript, and changes or errors may have been made by the journal's editor or copy editor, as well as Sage's copy editor, production editor, keyboarder, or designer. Read for typographical errors or any other correction necessary to the sense and accuracy of your article. Concurrent with your own review, your article is being proofread by Sage. We find, however, that many eyes are important, and we are counting on yours to help us publish your manuscript in its most accurate form.

If we have unanswered queries regarding your proofs, these will be noted in bold face type within the article itself. Please attend to these queries.

Figure 5.2. Sample Letter of Instructions Sent to Authors Along With Page Proofs

in order, you return the thing to the copy editor and that is the last you see of it until it appears in print. Using this approach, you never have the chance to examine the typeset version before it is published. This system is much more convenient for the *publisher's staff,* in that they do not have to go to all the trouble of mailing typeset page proofs back to the author

Figures: Shadow lines that may appear above or below your figure result from the copier; these will not be reproduced in your printed article.

Photographs: If your article contains photographs, a *copy* of the photo will appear with this notation to the printer: **FPO** (for position only). Ignore these notations. A halftone of the photograph itself will be made by the printer.

If your article contains math: We must ask that you assume responsibility for the correctness of equations and math terms. Please check for accuracy and the proper italics.

Mark your corrections on the proof set in a contrasting color. Red is preferred, but blue or green will do. Do not use black ink or pencil. Send your corrections in rather than phoning them in.

Please note: The proof review stage is not the time or the opportunity for rewriting. At this stage of production, every change costs time and money. If you make extensive revisions in the text, you will be charged at the rate of $2.00 per line. You will not, of course, be charged for any error introduced by someone else.

If we have not heard from you by the deadline noted above, we will assume that you have no changes, and we will move ahead to send this journal to press.

Please feel free to call if you have questions regarding these proofs. We greatly appreciate the time and attention you give your proof set, as well as your understanding of our time constraints.

Figure 5.2. Continued

(who may be in Costa Rica), waiting, prompting, and the like. Errors are more liable to creep into the manuscript, however, as your gimlet eye never has a chance to see that the typesetter didn't make any mistakes in transcription. Sure, an editor may have checked it after typesetting, but surely not with the loving thoroughness that you would have provided.

One final note about this: Some journals do not typeset their articles at all. Instead, authors are provided with detailed

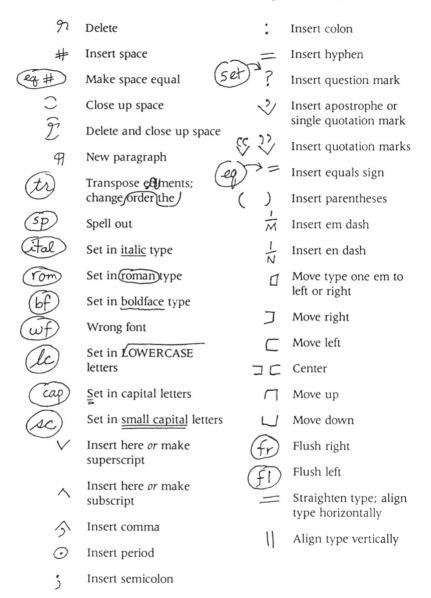

Figure 5.3. Some Commonly Used Proofreaders' Marks

SOURCE: Winchester, N., & Beebe, L. (1993). Production procedures (pp. 207-222). In L. Beebe (Ed.), *Professional writing for the human services.* Washington, DC: NASW Press. Copyright © 1993, National Association of Social Workers, Inc. Reprinted with the permission.

instructions on the correct formatting of an accepted article, and the publisher uses some sort of photocopying system to print the actual manuscripts as prepared by the authors (this is called working from camera-ready copy). These are assembled into journal issues, bound, and distributed. My subjective impression is that the journals that do this tend to be those of less prestige within a given field. After all, the subliminal message seemingly conveyed is that "your article is not important enough for us to bother with typesetting." In general, authors should resort to such journals only when they have gone down their list of prospective publications and have been rejected by those more reputable ones that do typeset articles.

Ordering Reprints

You will likely be given the option of ordering reprints of your article. If so, there will be a form sent to you to be filled out and returned with a check or purchase order number from your institution, made out to cover the cost of the quantity of reprints you order. If you order reprints, the publisher will arrange to print up a number of extra copies of your article, staple these together, and mail them to you. You can make use of these to respond to request for reprints from colleagues and to mail them out yourself to interested parties. Some publishers may provide you with a small supply (e.g., 25) gratis or instead send you one or more issues of the journal your article appeared in.

The cost of reprints is high, it seems to me. In certain fields wherein external funding has traditionally been available to purchase reprints, it may make sense to buy them. I have rarely done so. Instead, I make clean photocopies of the article, including all citation information, and keep a small supply of these on file. When I get requests for reprints or have other need for them, I use these neatly photocopied versions. You might want to ask your departmental chairperson or dean for institutional funds to pay for your reprints, but the availability of such monies is rare in these lean fiscal times. Act as your judgment and finances permit. If your article contains detailed photos, x-rays, positron emission tomography, or other images in which high-quality resolution is important, you may find that ordering a small quantity of reprints is particularly indicated. Actual reprints are also more desirable to include in promotion/tenure dossiers, as opposed to photocopies of articles.

Paying Publication Fees

When your article is accepted, you may also be hit with a bill for publication expenses. This is usually separate from an order form for reprints, although, as mentioned earlier, some journals combine the two in a mandatory reprint order policy. Some journal publishers have an *optional* publication charge. You are asked to pay it if and only if you have funding available to do so. Publication, however, is *not contingent* on payment of this fee. It is a more common practice, among those journals that levy publication fees, to make such payments a condition of publication. Treat these as any other bill or professional expense and pay them promptly via personal check or institutional purchase order (ask the dean?). Console yourself, if it has to come out of your own pocket, with the thought that such payments can likely be used as a deduction on this year's federal income taxes.

Once you have done the above, you can truly relax, basking in the knowledge of a job well done, and await the appearance in print of your groundbreaking study.

6 | Marketing Your Published Article

In literature, as in love, we are astonished at what is chosen by others.

—André Maurois

Now that your article has appeared in print in a rigorous, peer-reviewed journal where it will be listed in the relevant citation indices and abstracting services, and you are basking in the afterglow of a job well done, it is important to realize that you have a continuing parental obligation to your creation.

Send Your Work to Colleagues

Now, most active scholars are like you, in a continuous struggle to keep abreast of the latest developments in their disciplines. This remains a difficult undertaking, despite the availability of "journals" that publish nothing except book reviews or the citations and abstracts of recently published works in a given field. It is a professional courtesy on your part to send scholars active in your field a copy of your latest article pertaining to common research interests. This is not being presumptuous. To the contrary, most credible academics are more than pleased to have persons like yourself take the initiative in bringing relevant works to their attention. To send them copies is an extension of your role as one dedicated to disseminating knowledge in whatever field you have chosen for your life's work.

In addition, there is a less altruistic motive at work. If you send reprints of your recent publications to other scholars, they are more likely to cite you when they produce related works. We know that being cited by others is a useful benchmark of one's contributions to a field of scholarship, so attempting to maximize such citations by bringing your work to the attention of colleagues is a perfectly legitimate tactic. If your research has compelling practice or public policy applications, then practitioners, politicians, or governmental workers are also likely to be interested in receiving copies of your work. Please, have no qualms about proactively sending out copies of your reprints.

Send Your Work to the Mass Media

Each night the national news programs carry one or more stories based on an article that just came out in some major medical journal. These stories have sometimes been in production for some time but have been embargoed (publication in the mass media withheld until published in the scholarly journal). Many important discoveries are jointly covered in this manner, with some journals (e.g., *The New England Journal of Medicine* and *Science*) having full-time public relations staff dedicated to such tasks. In fact, if your work is sufficiently significant, you can send page proofs of your article to news services (television and radio networks, newspapers, national magazines such as *Time* or *Newsweek*) in the hope that they will be sufficiently interested to prepare a story about your new article. (See also Fox and Levin's, 1993, *How to Work With the Media*, in this series.)

Apart from distributing page proofs or reprints of your recently published article, you have several other options when it comes to disseminating your discoveries to the mass media. One is to prepare a press release, the most elementary way of contacting the media and one more likely to generate follow-up and a story than sending them a reprint of a hard-to-understand journal article. A press release generally takes the form of a one- to two-page double-spaced statement, ideally on institutional letterhead, and headed by a catchy title in caps or bold type. In the upper-right-corner, put a phrase like "FOR IMMEDIATE RELEASE" or "FOR RELEASE ON APRIL 1, 1994" to let reporters know when the information can be used. Note that stories in the mass media about your work or findings should not appear prior to journal publication (remember Pons and Flieschmann!). Use an attention-grabbing topic sentence and come to the point immediately. Fill in the details in subsequent paragraphs, avoiding jargon and overly technical language. Use short sentences and cover the essentials of *who, what, where, when, why,* and *how.* It is best to present only one idea per paragraph. Remember that you are writing for the lay public.

Your local university probably has a public relations department and the staff may be able to provide you with advice in the preparation and distribution of press releases. Alternatively, you can hire a graduate student in journalism or a commercial firm to prepare, format, and reproduce your press release. You may wish to send your press release and/or reprint to the mass media, local media, or specialty outlets like professional association newsletters. You can target only newspapers, radio, television, or popular magazines or target some combination of these. Professional association newsletters are often a good bet, as they are sometimes starved for interesting copy and convey the additional benefit of bringing your work to the attention of the larger disciplinary community. Table 6.1 displays the addresses of some of the more significant media outlets. It is a good idea to call ahead and find the name of the person to send your materials to, rather than using the generic heading *Attention: Science Editor* or something similar. Ask to speak to her, and let her know who you are and that you will be sending her a press release and so on in the next day or so and that you will be glad to talk with her about your article's findings after she has seen it.

Table 6.1 Addresses of Some Mass Media Outlets to Whom
Press Releases/Reprints Can Be Sent

Individual Newspapers and News Services

The Associated Press
Attention: Science (or whatever) News Editor
50 Rockefeller Plaza
New York, NY 10020

The Atlanta Journal & Constitution
Attention: Science (or whatever) News Editor
Atlanta Newspapers
72 Marrietta St., NW
Atlanta, GA 30303

The Baltimore Sun
Attention: Science (or whatever) News Editor
Calvert & Centre Streets
Baltimore, MD 21278

Chicago Tribune
Attention: Science (or whatever) News Editor
435 North Michigan Avenue
Chicago, IL 60611

Los Angeles Times
Attention: Science (or whatever) News Editor
Times Mirror Square
Los Angeles, CA 90053

The New York Times
Attention: Science (or whatever) News Editor
229 West 43rd Street
New York, NY 10036

St. Louis Post-Dispatch
Attention: Science (or whatever) News Editor
Pulitzer Publishing Company
900 North Tucker Boulevard
St. Louis, MO 63101

United Press International
World Headquarters
Attention: Science (or whatever) News Editor
1400 Eye Street, NW
9th Floor
Washington, DC 20005

Table 6.1 Continued

The Washington Post
Attention: Science (or whatever) News Editor
1150 15th Street, NW
Washington, DC 20071

Television Networks

ABC Network
Attention: Science News Editor
77 West 66th Street
New York, NY 10023

CBS Network
Attention: Science News Editor
51 West 52nd Street
New York, NY 10019

NBC Network
Attention: Science News Editor
30 Rockefeller Plaza
New York, NY 10112

Turner Program Services
Attention: Science News Editor
Box 105366
100 International Boulevard
Atlanta, GA 30348

Popular Magazines

Editor, *Chronicle for Higher Education*
1255 Twenty-third Street, NW
Washington, DC 20037

Discover Magazine
Attn: Behavioral (or Medical and so on) Sciences Editor
3 Park Avenue
New York, NY 10016

Invention and Technology
Attn: Behavioral (or Medical and so on) Sciences Editor
Forbes Building
60 Fifth Avenue
New York, NY 10011

(Continued)

Table 6.1 Continued

Omni Magazine
Attn: Behavioral (or Medical and so on) Sciences Editor
1965 Broadway
New York, NY 10023

Science
Attn: Behavioral (or Medical and so on) Sciences Editor
American Association for the Advancement of Science
1333 H Street, NW
Washington, DC 20005

Science News
Attn: Behavioral (or Medical and so on) Sciences Editor
1719 N Street, NW
Washington, DC 20036

Scientific American
Attn: Behavioral (or Medical and so on) Sciences Editor
415 Madison Avenue
New York, NY 10017

Smithsonian Magazine
Attn: Behavioral (or Medical and so on) Sciences Editor
900 Jefferson Drive
Washington, DC 20560

Time Magazine
Attn: Behavioral (or Medical and so on) Sciences Editor
Time and Life Building
Rockefeller Center
New York, NY 10020

The purpose of preparing and distributing press releases is to have a reporter/journalist learn enough about your work to be sufficiently interested as to pursue doing a story about it. Most times, nothing will come of your efforts. Sometimes, however, a journalist will prepare a story directly from the reprint or press release; other times, a reporter will contact you. This leads us into the area of being interviewed about your journal article.

If a reporter/journalist contacts you to do a story on your recent article/research, in most cases it can be a useful and enjoyable experience (unless you are being called by Mike Wallace or in response to Senator Proxmire's latest Golden Fleece award). Telephone interviews are the standard, as is tape-recording your conversation. Respond politely and honestly to the journalist's questions and do not be too self-conscious. Try not to make more of your work than is deserved, but do not let its implications/applications or other areas of interest be overlooked either. Offer to check the story/report for accuracy before publication, but be aware that most journalists do not allow you to edit their product. You may not even see it before it is printed/aired. This is common, so do not take umbrage. Also, it is unlikely that the journalist will send you a copy of his story about your article, so you will have to keep your eye open for it yourself. After the interview, if you have further thoughts, do not hesitate to recontact the journalist. After publication/airing, if you were pleased with the result, it is a good practice to call/write the journalist to thank him for his terrific work.

Respond to Requests for Reprints

You are likely to receive some requests for reprints of your article. It is very important that you respond promptly to these requests by sending either a typeset reprint of your article to the requestor or a clean photocopy (if you chose not to purchase reprints). It is not accepted practice to charge for this service, either for the reprint itself or for postage. Rather, this is commonly viewed as an ongoing obligation of the authors of scholarly works, part and parcel of the process of disseminating knowledge.

Provide Others With
Your Raw Data, if Requested

Although rare, you might be asked to provide others with access to your raw data, either in the form of a hard copy or on floppy disk. It is expected that the authors of scholarly works will comply with such requests promptly and positively and will be available for correspondence relating to the details of their research (see Bryant & Wortman, 1978; Eaton, 1984; Greenwald, 1976; Johnson, 1964; Stock & Kulhavy, 1989; Wolins, 1962). It is reasonable to charge for photocopying expenses or other costs in providing others with access to your raw data but not to seek to make a profit from such fees. Basically, any fees should cover expenses and no more. Although there are no hard-and-fast rules, it is a good practice for you to retain raw data, laboratory notebooks, computer diskettes and printouts, data analyses, and so forth for some time (perhaps up to 5 years?) following the publication of your article.

One alternative to cluttering up your office with spreadsheets, printouts, and disks containing data from previously published articles is to deposit your raw data, experimental protocols, and so on with the National Auxiliary Publications Services (NAPS), a service of the American Society for Information Science. These good folks will retain your materials indefinitely, carefully cataloged, and make it available to other scholars on request. Both you and the other scholars are charged a fee for this service, but it can be a great convenience, particularly for prolific writers with many studies to their credit. After depositing and registering your materials with NAPS, when you write your article, include a footnote in it stating where readers can obtain the raw data. You can write NAPS using the following address:

ASIS/NAPS
c/o Microfiche Publications
440 Park Avenue South
New York, NY 10016

One exception to the principle of providing others with access to your raw data is the case of information with significant commercial applications. This is a thorny issue for academics, less so for practitioners, as the dissemination ethic conflicts with proprietary concerns. But if you have published research on a new gene-splicing procedure, jointly developed at your university laboratory but being concurrently tested and marketed by a pharmaceutical company that has given you a sizable research grant in the hopes of developing a new effective treatment, the problems are obvious. Fortunately, for most professionals publishing in professional journals, they are rarely encountered.

Five years following the publication of my doctoral dissertation, a doctoral student at Florida State University, where I was teaching, developed a novel method of statistical analysis that he had applied to hypothetical data. He was in search of a set of real data and asked me if I would make mine available to him. I had retained my dissertation's raw data, printouts, and so forth, so I was both pleased and able to comply. He proceeded to reexamine my results using his new method of analysis and came up with conclusions at variance to my own. He used these data (crediting me with making them available, of course) in an article that he published in a leading social work journal, describing his statistical procedures, and using his different outcomes to tout the superiority of his method over those I applied. The editor of the journal invited me to prepare a "Response to Professor Jones"-type of article, which I was of course (!) pleased to do, and the two articles were published in tandem. So, quite apart from furthering additional scientific inquiries, my willingness to share raw data in this case resulted in another published article in a professional journal.

A related example of the importance of keeping one's raw data occurred while I was writing this chapter. Dr. Jeffrey Masson, *enfant terrible* of the psychoanalytic establishment, had sued Janet Malcolm, a journalist who published an article about him in a December 1983 issue of *The New Yorker*.

Dr. Masson alleged that Ms. Malcolm fabricated libelous and defamatory quotes from him. The case proceeded through the legal system and was recently decided on by the U.S. Supreme Court, in favor of Dr. Masson. Although Ms. Malcolm claimed that everything she wrote about Dr. Masson was true, and all material in quotation marks consisted of statements actually made by him, she had no documentation to back up the particulars of the quotes Dr. Masson was most incensed about. According to a story in *The Economist*, "Ms. Malcolm had recorded 40 hours of conversations. But some of her material was typed up from handwritten notes, which she later lost" (Staff, 1993, p. 32). Obviously, Dr. Masson's case would have been tossed out if she had been able to produce tape recordings of him making the supposedly libelous statements. Even handwritten notes prepared at the time would have been helpful. The moral here is to keep your data in good order, and for a long time, not only for scientific purposes but for legal ones as well.

Grant Requests to Reprint Your Work

You may be asked to provide permission for others to reprint all or part of your article in works (e.g., articles, books, chapters) of their own. For example, an editor of a new book may wish to include your entire article as a chapter of his or her work, or another scholar writing an article may want to reprint a table or figure or to quote a lengthy passage from your article in the new work. You may also receive requests from commercial photocopying concerns (e.g., Kinko's, Target Copy Centers) to include your article in coursepacks being prepared by other faculty. Etiquette requires that you respond to all such requests promptly, and my own view is that you should withhold permission only very rarely. For example, if you are preparing a book or collection of readings similar to that proposed by the requestor, and you had already planned to include your article in your own book, it would be reasonable to withhold permission for another to use your work for the same purpose in a competing text. Alternatively, the book editor requesting permission to reprint your article may be someone with an unfavorable reputation in your field, whom you do not want to be associated with, even in print. Perhaps the plan is for the requestor to print your article and have others criticize it in reaction papers, an arrangement that you are not comfortable with. So, although there are some situations when it is appropriate to withhold permission for other people to reprint your work, in general you will rarely encounter these. On the contrary, most often you should be very pleased to have your article further disseminated in this manner.

Usually the copyright to your work is held by the publisher of your journal, and apart from requestors having your permission to reprint your material, they must be referred to seek similar permission from the publisher, who may charge a fee for this service. It is not usually worth the trouble to try and receive any compensation for yourself in these matters. When the possibility presents itself, I usually grant such permissions gratis, even in the case of reproducing multiple copies, as in assembling coursepacks to be purchased by students. Any fees that would come to me originate from the pockets of the students purchasing the coursepacks (not the professor developing the coursepack), and I do not need the $20 to $30 that much. In general I try to place as few obstacles as possible in the path of other scholars who wish to use my journal articles for teaching purposes. It is a common practice for the editor or publisher of a book that includes a reprinted article of yours to send you a copy of the finished collection. Do not be shy about requesting such a copy, which should be provided to you without charge.

7 | Developing a Personal Program of Productive Publishing

Against the disease of writing one must take special precautions, since it is a dangerous and contagious disease.
—Peter Abelard

Quite apart from the nuts and bolts of preparing and submitting manuscripts suitable for publication in respected journals within your discipline, the problem of finding the time and energy to devote to writing, and of locating the resources necessary to undertake the scholarly research that is a precursor to such writing, often seems insurmountable to faculty. Consider too the plight of the practitioner, who, unlike her academic colleagues, is not expected or rewarded (if ever so meagerly) for publishing in professional periodicals. Such individuals share, perhaps to an even greater extent, the dilemma of finding the time and resources to write. In this final chapter I would like to present to you a variety of options that I have found useful in developing a productive program of professional writing, one that I have made use of over the past 14 years and that has proved very successful.

Consider Collaboration

In these increasingly interdisciplinary times, involving not only working with others in different fields but often using multiple sites for research and data collection, the image of the scholarly isolate, huddled alone in an office preparing his magnum opus, the definitive work in a particular area, one that will establish his reputation for all time as a careful researcher and respected authority, laboriously gestating, with the considered words ever so slowly creeping out from his pen, doesn't represent the modal form of contemporary scholarly endeavor. Indeed, the rise of multi-authored works, and a corresponding decline in single-authored ones, has been well documented in the psychological and social sciences. Unless you are a true misanthrope, work in a highly competitive field, and are liable to be "scooped" if you talk about your ideas with others, give careful thought to the possibility and advantages of working with others to jointly write journal manuscripts. Your choice of potential collaborators is quite large. Here are a few options that I have made good use of.

Students

Perhaps the biggest hurdle to my undertaking various writing projects is a lack of time: time to carefully review the literature, time to evaluate various potential measures for use in a study, time to format questionnaire protocols and surveys, time to gather data, time to score inventories and other forms of data, time to enter the information into a data-processing program, time to analyze it statistically and qualitatively, and so forth.

Now, I feel that the most important feature that I bring to a project is the ability to integrate theory with some state of affairs in the practical world that will bring about a test of one or more hypotheses derived from that theory. To do this requires some familiarity with the prior literature and theory, as well as competent skills as a research methodologist, these being needed to design studies in my fields. What I do not need is practice in tediously scoring inventories, entering data, and so on, and for such tasks I often recruit students.

As a faculty member I have constant opportunities to do this. My program offers bachelor's, master's, and Ph.D. degrees and I have potential access to students from all three levels. Students at each of these levels bring individual strengths that can be made use of in research and writing, and these skills do not necessarily correspond with the degree program they are enrolled in. Some of the very brightest ones I have worked with have been master's students, not Ph.D. matriculants, so in general I recruit such persons by virtue of their individual attainments, not degree program.

Degree programs in most disciplines offer some form of independent study wherein the student works closely with a faculty member (you?) on a project of mutual interest in return for academic credit. Often the end product is a lengthy paper prepared by the student. Honors theses, regular term papers, master's theses, doctoral dissertations, and various ad hoc projects all afford the opportunity for students to collaborate with you. When approached by students seeking such faculty mentoring, I almost always suggest that they undertake the type of intellectual effort necessary to prepare something of publishable quality, to put forth the extra energy needed to produce an enduring scholarly product, rather than a simple term paper likely relegated to the trash can once graded. Often I have five to six students concurrently working on various writing projects that I eventually hope to help them revise and submit as jointly authored journal articles.

The above approach has been an amazingly successful tactic. Of the last 50 articles I have published or have had accepted in scholarly journals, 29 were cowritten with students of mine. Many of these works could not have been attempted without the willing collaboration and diligent efforts of these talented persons. To be sure, I have had my share of incompetent students who failed to follow through on assigned tasks, were sloppy in their data collection, or were simply lazy. With proper supervision on my part, however, the large majority of them have proved to be valued collaborators to whom I owe an immense debt of gratitude and from whom I have learned a great deal. I cannot emphasize enough the valuable assistance that students can provide you in developing a credible track record as a scholar in your discipline. In addition, to some extent we members of the academy are expected to take promising scholars under our wing for a bit of individualized attention. Working with them, and ultimately being linked together in literary immortality as coauthors, is a fine way to implement this form of faculty responsibility.

Faculty Colleagues

For some reason, due no doubt to some personal foible of my own that intensive psychoanalysis would reveal, I have always found it easier to collaborate with my students than with my faculty colleagues. Remember those dreaded group assignments in school? There was always someone on your "team" who fumbled his task or who simply let the others carry him along, leaving you to pick up the slack at the last minute. Perhaps worse was the bossy person who, in a dictatorial manner, assumed managerial responsibility and abrasively directed everyone on what to do. Unfortunately, such individuals have their counterparts in academia, individuals with their own research agendas to prosecute, career timetables to consider, and personal axes to grind, not to mention personal psychopathology.

Nevertheless, when given lemons, make lemonade. Here are some specific approaches to undertaking collaborative efforts with faculty that can yield publishable journal manuscripts.

Offer to Assist the Established Scholar. A generally useful tactic, particularly for the novice faculty member and/or inexperienced writer, is to approach the leading lights in your department (or even college or university) and ask them, in effect, "Do you have any scholarly projects under way that I could help you with, and contribute to, to such an extent as to merit junior authorship when the project is completed?" Believe me, most active scholars will welcome you with open arms, as manna from heaven, as the answer to their prayers! They are almost always looking for bright, talented people just like you, who are amenable to supervision but capable of working independently, to assist in various projects. If the person answers in the affirmative, inquire further as to the nature of the project, time schedule, expectations from you in terms of time and resources, and so forth. Make up your mind. If you decide to proceed, full steam ahead. If the initial project described to you is unsuitable, gracefully decline but ask about any other potential activities.

Obviously it is more sensible to undertake relatively short-term and manageable projects with a colleague of unknown disposition (you will be surprised at how the most amiable soul turns into a raving lunatic when it comes to reasonable scholarly differences) and to bring them to a successful conclusion before signing on to a 3-year project of massive proportions. If one project is brought to fruition, the process can be repeated. Gradually you can begin creeping up the hierarchy of authors of multiauthored works to eventually emerge as the senior author (earned through increasingly greater responsibilities, of course), with the established scholar more toward the tail end of the list. Indeed, I think that this is a natural progression and an excellent way to learn the publishing game.

I followed this approach when I took a part-time clinical job at the Department of Psychiatry at the University of Michigan Medical School. I was initially affiliated through purely clinical activities with a productive group of psychiatrists and psychologists. I can't recall whether I was approached, or whether I approached one of them, but I soon found myself putting in lots of extra hours at the hospital, treating patients following experimental protocols, reviewing and summarizing literature, or gathering and analyzing data for studies that were designed by psychiatry faculty. I did this for free, in return for the promise of junior authorship on an article or two. My mentors were patient with my mistakes and over time gave me greater responsibilities. After a few years, I was designing studies for which I became the senior author and they were second, third, and fourth on the list. Meanwhile, they had other projects in the works that I was not involved in (they were collaborating with others, perhaps), and it turned out to be an amazingly productive and instructive 5 years for me, and for them as well. The model was clearly one of symbiosis and was largely responsible for my own enthusiasm for scholarly writing.

Help Others Draft or Revise Stalled Articles. It is likely that some of your colleagues are in a situation similar to one you have experienced, namely, having collected data on some scholarly project but not being able to find the time to work them up into a publishable manuscript. You can be of help to your colleagues who are faced with this dilemma by offering to take their otherwise useless data off their hands and draft that manuscript they have been meaning to prepare for so many months now.

Assuming that you have the time (and they do not) and the motivation (tenure decision coming up, "fire in the belly," and so on), you can be of great service to your peers by helping them get unstuck. *You* take the data, or assimilate the research, and *you* prepare the first draft. Many of us laggards, once we have something concrete in our hands, are very capable of revising and editing drafted material, but putting incisive words initially down on virgin paper is often considerably more difficult. Now, if you actually *write* significant portions of a manuscript, perhaps organize the presentation of the data, or even analyze it and draft the results section, then by any standard it would seem that you would merit junior authorship of such a paper. This is a win-win situation. Your colleague is helped by getting his or her ideas and prior hard work into print (which would not have been likely without your help), and you gain the additional skill and experience justifying another authorship.

Often you will hear a colleague lamenting that he (for example) has simply not been able to prepare an article that he has been gestating. At this point, with a solicitous smile, ask: "Can I help?" Ask to review the notes or data. Examine his materials. If they seem to contain a reasonable amount of credible data, pick up this conversation later on with your peer, saying: "You know, I think I could work up a draft for you on this project. Would you like me to do that?" If he answers in the affirmative, segue into the heart of the matter by asking, "Where do you think we could send it?" (Notice the operative word "we.") If he mentions one or more journals, reply, "Sounds good to me," if they are halfway reasonable choices, and begin your work. If he balks, then be more blunt about requesting junior authorship. If he still declines to share authorship, then reluctantly withdraw your offer to "help," leaving him with the remark that your offer will still be good in the future, if he changes his mind.

Now, don't just prepare a "first draft." Write a really competent article from title page to reference list. Word-process it, of course, and prepare the title page with your colleague as first author and you as second (or further down the list, as appropriate). Give him this "first draft" that, you hope, will not require too much further work on the senior author's part. The obvious effort you put into preparing the article should mollify any lingering reservations he may have in allowing you aboard this project. Because you have it on disk (and he does not), ask him to note any changes he wants on the manuscript and give it back to you to make the revisions. Repeat this process until both of you are satisfied with the work.

I always suggest that *you* assume responsibility for mailing the manuscript out for publication and list yourself as the corresponding author for all communications from the editor. The senior author can be listed as the contact person to whom requests for reprints or other correspondence should be directed *after* publication, but you should try and keep control of the submission process, because you know that you will respond promptly to correspondence, prepare a suitable revision, or resubmit it to another journal with a minimum of delay if it is rejected by your first-choice outlet. You just do not know if your colleagues will give the same careful attention to detail and prompt action to the manuscript as you will, hence my suggestion that you try to be in charge of this aspect of the publishing process. Ideally, this happy circumstance is arranged by the agreeable consensus of the other authors. After all, you are just trying to be helpful in relieving them of another annoying detail of academic life. If the senior or other authors insist on doing this themselves, smile agreeably and relinquish the matter. It is really not important enough to bicker over. Just check in with them periodically on the status of the article to make sure they have not fallen asleep at the switch.

A variation on this approach is to listen sympathetically as your colleague laments getting back a request for revision of an article, a revision that he is unable to get around to doing because of pressing administrative duties, teaching responsibilities, student advising, ill health, home problems, and so on. Step in with your eleemosynary proposition. If it is declined, smile agreeably and gently inquire, a couple of months later, if your friend has gotten his revision back to the editor.

Yet a third permutation of this tactic can occur when a faculty peer mentions having had a paper rejected by a journal. Wait a few months and ask if he or she has sent it out again. If not, ask if you could help take it off his or her hands by revising it appropriately and undertaking to get it published by sending it off to further journals, again with you as a junior author.

Ask Others to Help You. Now each of the above approaches to getting published can occur in the reverse. If *you* have data you've been unable to analyze and write up, consider judiciously asking a colleague to undertake these tasks, in return for junior authorship. If *you* have been unable to undertake a proper revision of an article and to resubmit it to the same journal, as the editor invited you to do, then ask a peer to help by doing this for you. The same is true for the rejected manuscript residing in a file drawer or one never even submitted. One of my doctoral students at Florida State did this with success, working both ends of the spectrum. She submitted a manuscript to a major journal and got a request to "revise and resubmit." This was done independently of me. When this decision arrived, she was in the middle of preparing for comprehensive examinations, dissertation, or something, and she spontaneously asked me if I would help prepare the revision, in return for junior authorship. I agreed, spent a *lot* of time on it (and made it into a much better article, I think), and we got it accepted with her as the senior author and me as the second. Sometime later, she spontaneously asked me if I had any old unpublished papers she could try to work up for submission. I went through my files and located an old graduate school term paper that I had always wanted to try and get published but had just never gotten around to. I handed it to her, with my best wishes. A few weeks later I got her revision back, which I edited and she later submitted to a second-rate journal. It was accepted, to our mutual delight.

Please note that I am not advocating taking advantage of anyone. Rather, I recommend joining forces and resources with colleagues who are stuck in a rut or accepting some assistance when you are stalled. This is perfectly moral, virtuous, credible, and right. I am most definitely not suggesting merely appending your name to the work of others and seeking authorship credit.

Practitioner Colleagues

All of the above methods of publishing can be implemented with practitioner colleagues. These would be persons active in your field who are not university based but are employed privately or in a public agency. Obviously the practice professions are most liable to possess a reservoir of such individuals, but often retired colleagues from the purely academic disciplines can be tapped along these lines. Many retire with unfinished projects, unanalyzed data, rejected manuscripts, or revisions hanging fire, and all afford scope for your industrious efforts at helping your friend get published. Within the past 3 years I have worked with a psychiatrist who directed a child and adolescent inpatient program, in preparing a manuscript presently under review on the histories of physical and sexual abuse among his patients; with a retired professor of social work in writing a book review covering a topic that was his life's work (although I had been invited to review the book, I invited his collaboration and we submitted it under joint authorship); and a director of psychology at a state residential home for kids with severe disabilities, with whom I have jointly written three different published articles on evaluating treatments. Each such case represented true collaboration, and each article would likely not have been written by either of us working alone.

Who Deserves Authorship?

The question of who deserves to be an author of an article, and of the order of seniority of multiauthored works, can be a contentious one. This is understandable, given the importance of such factors in the career progress of academic scholars. Those lacking sufficient attainments in scholarly publishing are likely to have difficulties being promoted and getting tenured. In leading universities it is not enough that you have *cowritten* a certain number of articles, it is expected that you be the *senior author* of a certain proportion or even the *sole author*. In the latter instance the awarding and ordering of authorship is a moot point, of course, but the ordering of multiauthored works can be a dicey arrangement. Somehow it is expected that the order of authorship should reflect the intellectual contributions of the writers, with the first author being the most significant contributor, the second somewhat less so, and so on down the line. Whether it is better to be the sixth author in an article appearing in a top-flight journal, or the first author of one published in an academic backwater publication is not readily answerable. I suspect the former, but this is by no means a definitive opinion.

The number and ordering of authorship can have an impact on the extent to which you get picked up by the various citation services. Some of them, such as the *Index Medicus*, only list the first few authors of an article, with the balance being relegated to the lumpen proletariate designated as *et al*. Someone looking up such a citation to a multiauthored work might never have the opportunity to realize that *you* were author number five of a landmark study.

Generally, I have found that, by arranging the authorship plan with collaborators *up front*, prior to beginning significant work on a project, disagreements on this subject can be avoided. It is also a good idea to decide where you plan to send a manuscript (i.e., to which journal) in advance of a project's completion to avoid potential conflicts on this topic as well.

With respect to determining who should be designated as an actual author of an article, there are some guidelines to consult. Here is what the *Publication Manual of the American Psychological Association* has to say on the matter:

> Authorship is reserved for persons who receive primary credit and hold primary responsibility for a published work. Authorship encompasses, therefore, not only those to do the actual writing but also those who have made substantial scientific contributions to a study. . . . Substantial professional contributions may include formulating the problem or hypothesis, structuring the experimental design, organizing and conducting the statistical analysis, interpreting the results, or writing a major portion of the paper. (APA, 1983, p. 20)

The concept of substantial professional contributions covers a multitude of sins, and you have considerable discretion in determining authorship. Obviously, departmental chair persons, deans, or laboratory directors do not automatically deserve authorship, and there have been several well-publicized cases in the press recently in which such people got into trouble based on their "authorship" of work done by academic tyros for whom they were responsible, papers that turned out to be poorly done or even fabricated.

Of course, if those lengthy discussions you have had with your boss contributed significantly, in *your* judgment, to the completion of a project, then you *are* at perfect liberty to list him or her as a coauthor (with his or her consent, obviously). It is obvious that a track record of coauthoring scholarly journals with your department head or dean will likely stand you in good stead when you are being evaluated for tenure, promotion, or a raise.

Conversely, it is grossly unfair to deny authorship to someone who truly deserves it by virtue of his or her intellectual contributions, such as a student who worked with you on a project. This applies even if authorship is of little conceivable value to the person in question, such as a college senior going to work at daddy's car dealership after graduation. If the student did the work, then the student deserves the credit. My own personal policy has been, when the question of authorship is doubtful, to be generous and award it to a student or colleague. I figure that in the grand scheme of things it is better to commit the error of overinclusiveness than to deny merited recognition to someone. In addition, such a policy helps to attract others to agree to collaborate with you, which is another positive consideration. I don't know of anyone who has gotten into trouble from being overly generous in awarding authorships, but I know of more than a few who earned the reputations of being pretty stingy or, even worse, of exploiting the work of others and of not giving them proper credit.

The various academic disciplines and professions will no doubt have their own views on the question of multiauthored articles and of who deserves authorship credit. Physicians, for example, could read articles on this topic by Caelleigh (1991) or Hugh (1986a, 1986b), and nurses could examine Nehring and Durham (1986). If in doubt, scratch around and find out what others in your field have written. The guidelines I have provided, and those listed in the APA *Publication Manual*, will also stand you in good stead.

Be aware that in some fields, such as the biomedical sciences, that the main author (typically the lab director or coordinator of a large research group) is last, after the senior author and other contributors. This is known colloquially as the "anchor" position and such a practice is used by some of the very best journals (e.g., *Science, Nature*). Accordingly, in a list of five authors, A, B, C, D, and E, the order of importance would be A = 1, E = 2, B = 3, and so on.

Consider Alternative Publication Options

Although the focus of this monograph has been on the preparation, submission, revision, and eventual publication of articles in peer-reviewed journals, the aspiring author has a much wider variety of publication options than this. I will describe a few of these below, some of which will appeal to the academic scholar, others to the practitioner. In no case will producing such works be of harm to your reputation as a writer. Indeed, by preparing and publishing a wide variety of scholarly contributions, if based on a sound foundation of original articles in peer-reviewed journals (not in lieu of!), the scope of your skills is even better demonstrated. I mention these also to give consideration to the novice writer unable or unwilling to undertake the comparatively massive efforts involved in the preparation of original scholarly articles and who may desire a less rigorous way to break into print, a sort of testing of the waters.

Consider Writing Book Reviews

Like most professionals, you probably read a fair number of journals in your field or at least peruse the abstracts in major ones to get a sense of the latest developments (after all, who has time to actually *read* entire articles)? Many professional journals, both large and small (including *Science*, published by the prestigious American Association for the Advancement of Science), print reviews of recent scholarly books considered to be of interest to the periodicals' readers. Where do these reviews come from? From people just like you! Individuals with academic or professional degrees in your discipline, from university-based faculty and from private practitioners, from folks with decades of experiences in a discipline and from graduate students immersed in the latest developments.

Most journals have a book review editor, someone in charge of coordinating the preparation of book reviews. This person constantly receives unsolicited (and some solicited) books related to her journal's subject matter, usually the newest releases in a field. She is responsible for determining if a given book is worthy of being reviewed (admittedly somewhat of a political decision) and of recruiting a competent person to write a professional review of it. This can be a headache for the book review editor—often she has too many books and not enough potential reviewers. An administrator in my department was recently appointed the book review editor of a social work journal and she has been deluged with books sent to her by pulsatile publishers anxious to obtain favorable reviews to promote book sales and text adoptions. She has been reduced to shanghaiing faculty in our department to crank out reviews for her, as she lacked a sufficiency of competent external people to prepare them.

The point is that journals are sometimes in dire need of people like you to review books for them. To break into this niche, all you need to do is the following. Find the names and addresses of the book review editors for the top journals in your field or those that you are most familiar with. Write these people a letter (no more than one page) offering to prepare book reviews for them. In a few sentences, describe your particular areas of interest and expertise and your academic and professional experience. Keep it short and sweet, and send it along with a current, neat, and clean copy of your résumé or curriculum vitae that outlines your attainments in greater detail. Forget the silly idea of a one-page CV; make it as long as it needs to be. In all likelihood, you will get a favorable response, and, if not, repeat the process with a fresh set of journals until you do. Ideally, the book review editor will send you a set of guidelines for preparing book reviews for her journal. Follow these exactly. If she doesn't, peruse some of the better reviews recently published in her journal and model yours after these. There are a number of articles that describe the nuts and bolts of preparing scholarly book reviews, and these can be consulted as well (e.g., Budd, 1982; Hoge & West, 1979; Klemp, 1981).

Soon you will get one or more books in the mail, with a request from the book review editor that you review them for her journal. Mostly likely there will be deadline, which should be adhered to! Examine the book—if it appeals to you and you believe that you are competent to review it, send a prompt acknowledgment along with a date by which you promise to have the review in the book review editor's hands. If you are unwilling to review it, return it promptly with a brief explanation, along with a sentence or two expressing your interest in reviewing other types of books.

Once you turn in your review, you should get a prompt acknowledgment and shortly thereafter word that it has been accepted. Almost all competent book reviews *are accepted for publication* with little revision. Once it appears in print, you may receive reprints of your review or at the very least a copy of the issue in which it appeared. It is a courtesy to send copies of your review, after it has been published, to the publisher and to the author(s)/editor(s) of the book you evaluated. Do this. Having completed one book review, write the book review editor a note of appreciation, thank her for the opportunity to review a book for her illustrious journal, and express your interest in doing this again (if true).

The benefits of writing book reviews are multiple. First, your field (the journal readership) obtains information about a potentially important new development (the book you reviewed). Meritorious books are promoted by your favorable appraisal and the readership advised to avoid those less worthy. Someone has to make such judgments. Why shouldn't it be you?

Second, you have tasted of the cup of journal publishing and found it refreshing. Your initial writing efforts have been strongly reinforced by success; you sent your review to your mom, and she called with congratulations; and your name has appeared in a leading periodical of your profession. You may experience people coming up to you at professional meetings and complimenting you on your review. Maybe the author of a work you reviewed favorably will write you a note of appreciation, something to be particularly treasured if she is a leading authority whose work you have admired for years. Also, not to be ignored is that fact that you have done the journal staff a favor by helping them maintain the quality of their book review section. It is just possible that the editor will remember your helpfulness when you happen to send her a manuscript for publication in the near future!

You can prepare a section on your vitae listing such book reviews that you have prepared, using the following format:

Book Reviews

Charme, A. B. (1994). A review of "Quantum Mechanics for the Masses" by N. Bohr. *Journal of Subatomic Particles, 14,* 117-119.

Dirac, P. D. (in press). A review of "Quarks, Quasars and Dark Matter" by S. Hawking. *Journal of Astrophysics.*

In the event that the journal for whom you have been asked to write a book review does not provide you with formal guidelines to assist in its preparation, Figure 7.1 provides an example of some fairly generic ones that can be followed.

GUIDELINES FOR PREPARING A BOOK REVIEW
FOR *RESEARCH ON SOCIAL WORK PRACTICE*

Thank you for agreeing to review a book for *Research on Social Work Practice*. Book reviews serve a useful function in the larger professional community by providing capsule summaries of new works in our field.

Prepare your review in strict conformity with current APA style guidelines. If you are not familiar with these, look them up before beginning to write! Place a short header in the upper-right-hand corner of each page, and a page number flush right 2 lines below the header. Do not right justify the right margin. Double-space *everything*—single- or triple-space nothing. Use the following format in beginning your review:

Gambrill, E. (1983). *Casework: A competency-based approach.* Englewood Cliffs, NJ: Prentice-Hall (448 pp., $32.50-hb, $17.75-pb, ISBN-0-1311-9446-1).

The author's last name first, then initial(s), year of publication, then title (underlined). This is followed by the city of publication, abbreviation of the state, and then the publisher. Then indicate the total number of pages in the book, its costs (hb = hardback, pb = paperback), and the all-important ISBN (this is found in the front of the book). With this number, any bookstore can order the book.

First provide a description of the purpose of the book and a general overview of it. You may wish to structure your review around the structure of the book itself, for example, by presenting the material of each chapter in turn. Note a number of the book's positive features and only then go into any criticism that you may have. Refrain from personal invective.

For the purposes of this journal, you should note the degree of empirical support that the text seems to be based on. If the author doesn't do it, make the distinction between unsupported opinions presented in the book, conceptual or theoretically derived material, and content solidly supported by top-quality empirical research.

As a general guideline, we would like our reviews to reinforce authors for basing their writing on empirical research and generally convey to the reader that information derived from such sources is more likely to be a source of reliable findings than books based on other sources of knowledge.

Describe what clear and compelling *applications* to social work practice may be derived from the book. Note the audiences that are appropriate

Figure 7.1. Sample Guidelines for Preparing a Book Review

potential readers (undergraduate students, experienced practitioners, researchers, policy analysts, and so on) and any uses to which the book is especially appropriate (advanced practice classes, adoption agencies, private practitioners, and so on).

Complete your review by noting your name, position, and affiliation, as follows, all flush right:

Mary Richmond
Professor
Columbia University School of Social Work

or

Mary Richmond
Clinical Social Worker
Georgia Mental Health Institute

When you are finished with your review, please word process it and mail four very clean copies to the Book Review Editor—*RSWP*, Denise Bronson, Ph.D., College of Social Work, Ohio State University, Columbus, Ohio 43210. Use a laser printer, if possible. Also include a signed and dated copy of the Sage Copyright form. The cover letter accompanying your review should include a statement to the effect that your review represents original and previously unpublished material that is not under concurrent editorial review.

It is possible that Dr. Bronson may request some revisions to your review. Please complete these as soon as possible and submit a revision. When your review is published, Sage Publications, Inc., will send you a copy of the issue of the journal that contains your review. Etiquette suggests that you send two copies of your review to the senior author of the book you reviewed and to the publisher (Attn: Marketing Department). They may wish to include some statements from your review in their future advertising. If the book is good, and you say so, we reinforce the publication of quality books in our field. If the book is not very good, and you say so, both publishers and authors may be encouraged to do a better job next time.

Again, please accept our thanks for undertaking a book review for *Research on Social Work Practice*.

Figure 7.1. Continued

Keep your eyes open for "Lists of Books Received" that are published in some journals. If one or more of the titles listed is up your alley, write the book review editor and offer to review it. Conversely, if you have recently read, on your own, a particularly worthwhile professional book, consider writing to the book review editor with an offer to review this new book. She doesn't even need to send it to you. I recently did this in regard to a fine biography of Charles Darwin, written by John Bowlby, who applied some of his own psychological theories to the nature and etiology of Darwin's lifelong ill health. Bowlby's book was a terrific read and I was moved to ask the editor of a psychology journal if she'd like a book review. The answer was affirmative and the review has been published.

Respond to Published Articles

Haven't you had the experience of reading an article in one of your professional journals and of saying to yourself, "Those idiots, they didn't control for the possibility that . . . [fill in the blank]," or "What a fool, he completely ignored Funkenpoop's prior work in this field! I wonder if he even knows about Funkenpoop's studies?" Such experiences are golden opportunities to contribute, albeit in a small way, to your discipline's literature by submitting a letter for possible publication in response to a recently published article. Your comments should always, of course, be civil, and purely laudatory letters are of little interest or value to readers, but if a study had a major flaw, or the author appeared to be unfamiliar with earlier related studies of seminal value to his recently published article, then it is worthwhile to prepare a response to such recently published works and to submit it for publication yourself. Many of the leading journals provide opportunities for readers to exchange commentary with authors, and the interchanges are often fascinating and sometimes even constructive.

Similar benefits may accrue to letters to the editor that are not prepared in response to recent articles but may be a general observation about the direction the journal or the field has been taking. Other journals encourage letters as a form of communicating novel findings or preliminary results. Medical journals do this a great deal, and every so often some bizarre clinical observation that found its way into print as a letter to the editor in *The New England Journal of Medicine* hits the mass media. Many areas of inquiry have gotten their start by originally appearing in the form of a letter published in a journal. This can be a particularly functional manner for practitioners to break into print, because journals are at the forefront of practice in various fields, and the short, succinct format of letters to the editor is a very nonintimidating way to begin a writing program. Few resources are required beyond a careful writing style and access to a keyboard. Of course, it still pays to have a colleague review your work and give it a critical editing before sending it off. If you undertake this publishing option, add it to your vitae as follows:

Flinch, C. B. (1994). A response to "The Nebbish Hypothesis" (letter). *Journal of Unbridled Speculation, 13*, 6-5.

or

Broak, I. B. (1994). Problems in bill collection from patients with multiple personality disorder: Three case reports (letter). *Medical Practice Management, 23*, 63.

Write Editorials

Journals in some fields, particularly practice-type journals, often allocate publication space to printing editorials submitted by the readership. More lengthy than letters to the editor, editorials afford you the scope to vent your spleen or (more constructively) to add to disciplinary dialogue about some contemporary issue in your field. Sometimes editorials deal with political matters, how national initiatives affect your field, or perhaps intradisciplinary concerns. Although editorials are most often written by the editors of journals, who take advantage of their position to regularly inflict their personal views on the hapless readership, a carefully reasoned editorial that appears unsolicited on her desk, written by an informed reader such as yourself, may be given consideration for publication. If submitted and accepted, consider the following format for your vitae:

> Greade, I. M. (1994). National health care and reimbursement for psychological services (editorial). *Journal of Proprietary Psychology, 3,* 2-6.

Serve on Editorial Boards

Journals are able to operate largely because of the willingness of members of a given profession to serve as keepers of the gates of publication. There are several levels of such gatekeeping. The editor-in-chief (or simply the editor) of a journal is usually the ultimate arbitrator, but he or she is aided by a large cadre of helpers called "The Editorial Board." Most journals have an editorial board, and at a minimum these are persons who are invited to serve as regular reviewers of manuscripts submitted to a particular journal. Some journals have editorial board members assist in forming journal policies and practices, and some may have a separate advisory group for this purpose. Given journals may only use members of their own editorial boards to review manuscripts; other journals invite other persons, called ad hoc or guest reviewers, to add their views as well.

Ideally, persons invited to serve on editorial boards possess several attributes. They should have credible academic qualifications (usually the doctorate) in their field, be reasonably experienced/knowledgeable in the area to which the journal is dedicated, have a respectable track record of personally publishing in professional journals, and have a track record of preparing high quality reviews of manuscripts and of turning them in on time. Guest reviewers should possess similar qualifications. (Of course, sometimes individuals are appointed to editorial boards on the basis of who they know, or what personal attributes they may possess, rather than of having demonstrated a credible track record of journal publishing themselves, but we shall ignore this quirk in the system for the purposes of this discussion.)

Obviously, such talented individuals are at a premium in many fields, which leads us back to the opportunities this system has for you. I suggest that a useful tactic is to write a brief cover letter to the editors of the major journals that you make use of and offer to serve the journal as a guest reviewer. Clearly describe the areas of your discipline you are expert in so that the editor knows what types of manuscript are suitable for you to review. Send a neat, clean, and organized copy of your vitae along with the letter. This vitae should describe your degrees, the discipline in which they were awarded, dates they were earned, and the universities/colleges that awarded them. List your past and present academic and practice positions, including the inclusive dates each appointment was held. If you have any prior publications, list them on the vitae, using the publication style appropriate to your discipline. Sit back and wait.

You should receive a prompt acknowledgment of your offer and at some point be given a manuscript to evaluate, along with instructions for reviewers. Prepare your review (typed, of course) and submit it to the editor on time. After a few months, you should be informed of the editor's disposition of the manuscript, and you may be asked to rereview it, if a revision was submitted by the author(s). Once you have done this, add a section to your vitae and list those journals for which you have served as a guest reviewer—perhaps like this:

Editorial Duties
Guest Reviewer, 1994   *Journal of Praxics*
Editorial Board Member, 1994   *Proctology Digest*

You can see where this is going. Once you have competently guest reviewed a number of articles for a given journal, write the editor, remind her of your exertions on behalf of the journal, and ask that she consider appointing you to the editorial board when a vacancy occurs (this happens frequently due to deaths, incompetence, lack of interest, changing priorities, and so on). If you follow this approach concurrently for a number of journals, you should soon (within a couple of years) find yourself a member of one or more editorial boards, with all the attendant duties and privileges thereof.

Of course, such editorial board membership is a mark in your favor during promotion/tenure deliberations. Because aspirants for higher academic rank are expected to have regional (associate professor) or national/international (full professor) recognition, it is often assumed by university review committees that editorial board membership is a hallmark of such recognition, particularly for the more respectable journals in your field. Even service on second-rate journals' editorial boards is probably an asset in this regard.

The extra work that serving on editorial boards entails is partially offset by the insight it provides you into the journal publication system and the advance look at what may be forthcoming in your field. Moreover, you learn what the characteristics are of manuscripts likely to be accepted by a given journal, and what some of the pitfalls may be. This too is good. Perhaps more to the point of this monograph, editorial board service accrues good karma, merit if you will. When *you* submit a manuscript to the editor of a journal that you have diligently served for a couple of years, to the extent that editorial discretion is operative, you have maximized it to work in your favor. You cannot expect your article to be accepted automatically. It will (and should be) peer-reviewed, and you will get feedback and a decision. However, even quite negative feedback from reviewers can be responded to by the editor inviting you to prepare a revision along the indicated lines and to resubmit your work, in contrast to the simple rejection a person unknown to the editor might have received, given the same set of reviews. Here is where editorial discretion comes in, and it can be a powerful ally in your efforts to get published, *if* you lay the groundwork in advance. This will not work (and should not work) to your advantage in getting a piece of dreck published, but it can help in borderline decisions. Yes, this tactic could be considered opportunistic, but consider that you are not asking for something for nothing. You will have *earned* any consideration extended to you by an editor. You can rest assured that your colleagues are following this route, and in the long run it is a very functional approach, both for your career and for the benefit of your discipline.

Guest Edit Special Issues

Although this varies by field and by journal policy, sometimes journals publish "special issues," a thematically related collection of articles that *you* solicit, edit, and accept for publication on behalf of the journal. Take a look at the journals in your field and see if some of them do this. If so, consider writing the editor and nominating yourself to guest edit an entire issue devoted to some topic, preferably one with which you have demonstrable expertise. In your cover letter, describe the qualifications that you possess along these lines and provide some indication of your capacity to successfully recruit sufficient submissions to fill an entire issue. Send along your vitae, and await a response from the editor. If he declines, extend a similar offer to the editor of another journal that makes a practice of producing special issues. Repeat as needed. Eventually you may be successful. At this point, begin soliciting manuscripts. Perhaps the editor would let you run an announcement, a call for papers, in a regular issue of the journal, describing the thematic special issue and directing authors to send manuscripts for consideration in this issue to you (giving your address). You can also place such calls for papers in one or more professional newsletters and draw up a nice flyer and send it to graduate departments/professional schools in your field, asking that it be posted on public bulletin boards. Electronic bulletin boards are an increasingly useful venue in this regard, that is, publicizing calls for papers.

Sit back and await the flow of manuscripts. You will have come to an agreement with the regular editor as to how these will be processed (i.e., using the editorial board, using special guest reviewers, making the selection decisions yourself, and so on), and you will begin the review of these submissions. Over time you will assemble a collection of suitable manuscripts, obtain signed authors' agreements, diskettes, glossy prints, and so on and eventually send off a package of acceptable manuscripts to the editor, keeping, of course, within the page limitations he or she established.

Where this endeavor affords an opportunity for you is the chance of using this special issue to insert one or more manuscripts that *you* have written into the review process. Remember, *you* are the editor now, you have the discretion, you make the decisions, you decline and accept manuscripts! Power at last!

Now, realistically, you would not consider abusing your position to attempt to publish an article that falls short of the high standards set by the journal you are guest editing. In any event, the editor would likely screen out substandard work, because the reputation of his or her journal (and indirectly his or her own professional standing) is to some extent dependent on the quality of what is published during his or her tenure as editor. Nevertheless, the guest editing of a special issue of a professional journal does afford a natural opportunity for you to have one or more of your own fine studies published. Indeed, a perusal of guest-edited issues reveals that such is a very common practice. I have used this tactic myself to edit two special issues of different peer-reviewed journals and one special section of another journal's issue. Each yielded useful contributions to the professional literature to which I am proud to assign my name.

Summary

In this chapter I have reviewed some tactics useful in helping you develop a personal program of scholarly writing. Included were an examination of the benefits of collaborating with students, faculty colleagues, and practitioners; a look at differing publication media, such as book reviews, responses to articles recently published, letters to the editor, and editorials; and how to be invited to assume various editorial duties for journals, such as being a guest reviewer, joining editorial boards, and guest editing special issues of journals. Each of these tactics requires a degree of assertiveness, of chutzpa if you will, but each is also a very reasonable endeavor. Offering your services to others cannot be but helpful and appreciated. If at the same time you are assisted in publishing in scholarly journals, so much the better.

Concluding Remarks

For good or ill (mostly good in my opinion), the ever-expanding network of scholarly journals is the primary means of disseminating advances in the knowledge base of both academic disciplines and the professions. To become a part of this process through the medium of having written published articles is both a privilege and a challenge. As a university-based academic and a practitioner of a profession, I have had the opportunity to engage in classroom instruction and supervision of students at the undergraduate, master's, and doctoral levels. I have also enjoyed professional practice with clients experiencing various problems in living and mental/behavioral disturbance. I have found the art and science of journal publishing to be one of the most enjoyable aspects of my career. Through collaboration with students, my research and scholarship involves considerable teaching, and the readership of the journals in which I publish extends the scope of my pedagogical contributions. Through collaboration with colleagues, I help in the building of their careers and in enhancing the reputation of our departments. In working with practitioners, we produce clinical-research articles of benefit to the clients and patients of human service agencies.

By submitting one's work to the critical scrutiny of blind peer review, and publishing it for members of the profession to evaluate, one is helped to keep fresh and at the cutting edge of disciplinary developments. My hope is that, by reading this monograph, you have been positively stimulated to undertake efforts at publishing in scholarly journals and that you found some practices to emulate that will assist you in this endeavor. I encourage readers to send me comments and other useful ideas designed to promote excellence in journal publishing for inclusion in a future edition.

APPENDIX

Selected Disciplinary Writing Style Guides

Agronomy

American Society of Agronomy, Crop Science Society of America, and Soil Science Society of America. (1976). *Handbook and style manual.* Madison, WI: Author.

Biology

CBE Style Manual Committee. (1983). *CBE style manual: Guide for authors, editors and publishers in the biological sciences* (5th ed.). Bethesda, MD: Author.

Botany

Eichler, H. (1977). *Guidelines for the preparation of botanical taxonomic papers.* Melbourne, Australia: Commonwealth Scientific and Industrial Research Organization.

Chemistry

Dodd, J. S. (1986). *The ACS style guide: A manual for authors and editors.* Washington, DC: American Chemical Society.

NOTE: Guides to journal resources such as the above are constantly being updated. Authors should obtain the most recent edition of the guide to journals relevant to one's discipline and be guided accordingly.

Education

National Education Association. (1966). *NEA style manual for writers and editors.* Washington, DC: Author.

Engineering

Michaelson, H. B. (1986). *How to write and publish engineering papers and reports* (2nd ed.). Philadelphia, PA: ISI Press.

Geology

U.S. Geological Survey. (1978). *Suggestions to authors of the reports of the United States Geological Survey* (6th ed.). Washington, DC: Government Printing Office.

Humanities

Modern Humanities Research Association. (1991). *MHRA style book: Notes for authors, editors and writers of theses.* London: Author.
Wiles, R. M. (1977). *Scholarly reporting in the humanities* (4th ed., rev.). Toronto, Ontario: University of Toronto Press in association with the Humanities Research Council of Canada.

Law

Harvard Law Review Association. (1981). *A uniform system of citation* (13th ed.). Cambridge, MA: Author.

Mathematics

American Mathematic Society. (1980). *A manual for authors of mathematical papers* (7th ed.). Providence, RI: Author.

Medicine

Barclay, W. R., Southgate, T., & Mayo, R. W. (1981). *Manual for authors and editors: Editorial style and manuscript preparation* (7th ed.). Los Altos, CA: Lange Medical Publications.

International Committee of Medical Journal Editors. (1982). Uniform requirements for manuscripts submitted to biomedical journals. *Annals of Internal Medicine, 96,* 766-770.

Iverson, C., et al. (Eds.). (1989). *American Medical Association manual of style* (8th ed.). Baltimore, MD: Williams & Wilkins.

Microbiology

American Society for Microbiology. (1987). Instructions to authors for all ASM journals. *ASM News, 53,* i-xv.

Modern Languages

Achtert, W. S., & Gibaldi, J. (1985). *The MLA style manual.* New York: Modern Language Association of America.

Modern Language Association. (1977). *MLA handbook for writers of research papers, theses and dissertations.* New York: Author.

Organizational Science

Cummings, L. L., & Frost, P. J. (1985). *Publishing in the organizational sciences.* Homewood, IL: Irwin.

Physical Therapy

American Physical Therapy Association. (1976). *Style manual: Physical therapy; Journal of the American Physical Therapy Association* (4th ed.). Washington, DC: Author.

Physics

Hathwell, D., & Metzner, A. W. K. (Eds.). (1978). *Style manual for guidance in the preparation of papers for journals published by the American Institute of Physics* (3rd ed., rev.). New York: American Institute of Physics.

Political Science

American Political Science Association. (1988). *Style manual for political science.* Washington, DC: Author.

Psychology

American Psychological Association. (1983). *Publication manual of the American Psychological Association* (3rd ed.). Washington, DC: Author.

Social Work

Beebe, L. (Ed.). (1993). *Professional writing for the human services.* Washington, DC: NASW Press.

Sociology

Sussman, M. B. (1978). *Author's guide to journals in sociology and related fields.* New York: Haworth.

General

Butcher, J. (1981). *Copy-editing: The Cambridge handbook* (2nd ed.). New York: Cambridge University Press.

The Chicago manual of style (14th ed.). (1993). Chicago, IL: University of Chicago Press.

Day, R. A. (1988). *How to write and publish a scientific paper* (3rd ed.). New York: Oryx.

Howell, J. B. (1983). *Style manuals of the English-speaking world: A guide.* Phoenix, AZ: Oryx.

Longyear, M. (Ed.). (1983). *The McGraw-Hill style manual: A concise guide for writers and editors.* New York: McGraw-Hill.

Luey, B. (1991). *Handbook for academic authors* (rev. ed.). New York: Cambridge University Press.

Selected Disciplinary Journal Guides

Business

Kurtz, D. L., & Spitz, A. E. (1974). *An academic writer's guide to publishing in business and economic journals* (2nd ed.). Ypsilanti: Eastern Michigan University, Bureau of Business Services and Research.

Communication

Knapp, M. L., & Daly, J. A. (1993). *A guide to publishing in scholarly communication journals* (2nd ed.). Austin, TX: International Communication Association.

Economics

Cabell, D. W. (Ed.). (1988). *Cabells directory of publishing opportunities in business and economics* (4th ed.). Beaumont, TX: Cabell.

Education

Krepel, W. J., & DuVall, C. R. (1977). *Education and education-related serials: A directory.* Littleton, CO: Libraries Unlimited.
Levin, J. (1983). *Getting published: The educator's resource book.* New York: ARCO.

Engineering

Balachandran, S. (1982). *Directory of publishing sources: The researcher's guide to journals in engineering and technology.* New York: Wiley-Interscience.

Family Studies

Hanks, R. S., Matocha, L., & Sussman, M. B. (Ed.). (1992). *Publishing in journals on the family: A survey and guide for scholars, practitioners and students.* Binghamton, NY: Haworth.

History

Steiner, D. R. (1981). *Historical journals: A handbook for writers and reviewers.* Santa Barbara, CA: ABC-Clio.

Information Science

Stevens, N. D., & Stevens, N. B. (Eds.). (1982). *Author's guide to journals in library and information science.* New York: Haworth.

Law

Mersky, R. W., Berring, R. C., & McCue, J. K. (1979). *Author's guide to journals in law, criminal justice, & criminology.* New York: Haworth.

Literature

Harmon, G. L., & Harmon, S. M. (1974). *Scholar's market: An international directory of periodicals publishing literary scholarship.* Columbus: Ohio State University Libraries.

Medicine

Meiss, H. R., & Jaeger, D. A. (1980). *Information to authors, 1980-1981: Editorial guidelines reproduced from 246 medical journals.* Baltimore, MD: Urban & Schwarzenberg.

Nursing

Binger, J. L., & Jensen, L. M. (1980). *Lippincott's guide to nursing literature: A handbook for students, writers, and researchers.* Philadelphia, PA: J. B. Lippincott.

Warner, S. D., & Schweer, K. D. (1982). *Author's guide to journals in nursing and related fields.* New York: Haworth.

Philosophy

Moulton, J. M. (1975). *Guidebook for publishing philosophy* (2nd ed.). Newark, DE: American Philosophical Association.

Political Science

Political and social science journals: A handbook for writers and reviews. (1983). Santa Barbara, CA: ABC-Clio.

Psychology

American Psychological Association. (1990). *Journals in psychology: A resource listing for authors* (3rd ed.). Washington, DC: Author.

Wang, A. Y. (1989). *Authors guide to journals in the behavioral sciences.* Hillsdale, NJ: Lawrence Erlbaum.

Social Work

Mendelsohn, H. N. (1982). *An author's guide to social work journals* (3rd ed.). Washington, DC: NASW Press.

Sociology

Huber, B. J. (1982). *Publishing options: An author's guide to journals, 1982.* Washington, DC: American Sociological Association.
Rhoades, L. D. (Ed.). (1974). *The author's guide to selected journals.* Washington, DC: American Sociological Association.
Sussman, M. (1978). *Author's guide to journals in sociology and related fields.* New York: Haworth

General

Directory of publishing opportunities in journals and periodicals (5th ed.). (1981). Chicago: Marquis Academic Media.
Lyle, S. P. (1979). Authors' guides to scholarly periodicals. *Scholarly Publishing, 10,* 255-261.
Lyle, S. P. (1984). Authors' guides to scholarly periodicals. *Scholarly Publishing, 15,* 273-279.

References

American Psychological Association. (1983). *Publication manual of the American Psychological Association* (3rd ed.). Washington, DC: Author.

Beebe, L. (Ed.). (1993). *Professional writing for the human services.* Washington, DC: NASW Press.

Broad, W. J. (1988, February 16). Science can't keep up with flood of new journals. *The New York Times,* pp. C1, C11.

Bryant, F. B., & Wortman, P. M. (1978). Secondary analysis: The case for data archives. *American Psychologist, 33,* 381-387.

Budd, J. (1982). Book reviewing practices of journals in the humanities. *Scholarly Publishing, 13,* 363-371.

Caelleigh, A. (1991). Credit and responsibility in authorship. *Academic Medicine, 66,* 676-677.

Cicchetti, D. V. (1991). The reliability of peer review for manuscript and grant submissions: A cross disciplinary investigation. *Behavioral and Brain Sciences, 14,* 119-135.

Close, F. (1991). *Too hot to handle: The race for cold fusion.* Princeton, NJ: Princeton University Press.

Cripa, B. (1993). One climber got there first. *Science, 260,* 1424-1425.

Cullen, D. J., & Macauley, A. (1992). Consistency between peer reviewers for a clinical specialty journal. *Academic Medicine, 67,* 856-859.

Day, R. A. (1988). *How to write and publish a scientific paper* (3rd ed.). New York: Oryx.

Diamond, A. M. (1986). What is a citation worth? *Journal of Human Resources, 21,* 200-215.

Eaton, W. O. (1984). On obtaining unpublished data for research integration. *American Psychologist, 39,* 1325-1326.

Eberley, S., & Warner, W. K. (1990, Fall). Fields or subfields of knowledge: Rejection rates and arguments in peer review. *American Sociologist*, pp. 217-230.

Epstein, W. M. (1990). Confirmational response bias among social work journals. *Science, Technology, & Human Values, 15*, 9-38.

Euster, G. L., & Weinbach, R. W. (1983). University rewards for faculty community service. *Journal of Education for Social Work, 19*, 108-114.

Feingold, A. (1989). Assessment of journals in social science psychology. *American Psychologist, 44*, 961-964.

Fox, J. A., & Levin, J. (1993). *How to work with the media* (Vol. 2, Survival Skills for Scholars). Newbury Park, CA: Sage.

Friman, P. C., Allen, K. D., Kerwin, M. L. E., & Larzelere, R. (1993). Changes in modern psychology: A citation analysis of the Kuhnian displacement thesis. *American Psychologist, 48*, 658-664.

Fry, D. M., Walters, G., & Schuerman, L. E. (1985). Perceived quality of fifty selected journals: Academicians and practitioners. *Journal of the Academy of Marketing Science, 13*, 352-361.

Garfield, E. (1988). *The SSCI journal citation reports*. Philadelphia, PA: Institute for Scientific Information.

Giroux, R. (1982). *The education of an editor*. New York: Bowker.

Greenwald, A. G. (1976). An editorial. *Journal of Personality and Social Psychology, 33*, 1-7.

Hargens, L. L. (1988). Scholarly consensus and journal rejection rates. *American Sociological Review, 53*, 139-151.

Hoge, J. O., & West, J. L. (1979). Academic book reviewing: Some problems and suggestions. *Scholarly Publishing, 11*, 35-41.

Holt, M. E. (1988). Editorial: Reflections on scholarly publications. *Innovative Higher Education, 13*(1), 3-10.

Howard, G. S., Cole, D. A., & Maxwell, S. E. (1987). Research productivity in psychology based on publication in the journals of the American Psychological Association. *American Psychologist, 42*, 975-986.

Hugh, E. J. (1986a). Abuses and uses of authorship. *Annals of Internal Medicine, 104*, 266-267.

Hugh, E. J. (1986b). Guidelines on authorship of medical papers. *Annals of Internal Medicine, 104*, 269-274.

Huizenga, J. R. (1992). *Cold fusion: The scientific fiasco of the century*. Rochester, NY: University of Rochester Press.

Johnson, R. W. (1964). Retain the original data. *American Psychologist, 19*, 350-351.

Kirk, S. A., & Corcoran, K. J. (1989). The $12,000 question: Does it pay to publish? *Social Work, 34*, 379-381.

Klemp, P. J. (1981). Reviewing academic books: Some ideas for beginners. *Scholarly Publishing, 12*, 135-139.

Koulack, D., & Keselman, H. J. (1975). Ratings of psychology journals by members of the American Psychological Association. *American Psychologist, 30,* 1049-1053.

Lake, R. H., & Doke, E. R. (1987). Marketing journal hierarchies: Faculty perceptions, 1986-1987. *Journal of the Academy of Marketing Science, 15,* 74-78.

Lindsey, D. (1978). *The scientific publication system in social science.* San Francisco: Jossey-Bass.

MacReynolds, P. (1971). Reliability of ratings of research papers. *American Psychologist, 25,* 400-401.

Mattaini, M. A. (1993). *More than a thousand words: Graphics for clinical practice.* Washington, DC: NASW Press.

Mendelsohn, H. N. (1992). *An author's guide to social work journals* (3rd ed.). Washington, DC: NASW Press.

Nederhof, A. J. (1989). Books and chapters are not to be neglected in measuring research productivity [Letter]. *American Psychologist, 44,* 734-735.

Nehring, W., & Durham, J. (1986). Multiple authorship and professional advancement. *Dimensions of Critical Care Nursing, 5,* 58-62.

Neuliep, J. W., & Crandell, R. (1993). Reviewer bias against replication research. *Journal of Social Behavior and Personality, 8,* 21-29.

Niemi, A. W. (1988). Research productivity of American business schools. *Review of Business and Economic Research, 23,* 1-17.

Novak, J. S. (1988). *Enhancing Lamaze techniques.* Los Angeles: The Body Press.

Peery, J. C., & Adams, G. R. (1981). Qualitative ratings of human development journals. *Human Development, 24,* 312-319.

Peters, D. P., & Ceci, S. J. (1982). Peer-review practices of psychological journals: The fate of published articles submitted again. *Behavioral and Brain Sciences, 5,* 185-197.

Rothman, M. A. (1990). Cold fusion: A case history in "wishful science"? *The Skeptical Inquirer, 14*(2), 161-170.

Scott, W. A. (1974). Interreferee agreement on some characteristics of manuscripts submitted to the *Journal of Personality and Social Psychology. American Psychologist, 29,* 698-702.

Seiler, L. H. (1989, September). The future of the scholarly journal. *Academic Computing,* pp. 14-16, 66-69.

Spencer, N. J., Hartnett, J., & Mahoney, J. (1985). Problems with reviews in the standard editorial practice. *Journal of Social Behavior and Personality, 1,* 21-36.

Staff. (1993, June 12). Pen versus tape. *The Economist,* p. 32.

Stinchcombe, A. L., & Ofshe, R. (1969). On journal editing as a probabilistic process. *American Sociologist, 4,* 116-117.

Stock, W. A., & Kulhavy, R. W. (1989). Reporting primary data in scientific articles: Technical solutions to a perennial problem [Letter]. *American Psychologist, 44,* 741-742.

Taubes, G. (1993). Measure for measure in science. *Science, 260,* 884-886.

Thyer, B. A., & Bentley, K. J. (1986). Academic affiliations of social work authors: A citation analysis of six major journals. *Journal of Social Work Education, 22,* 67-73.

Tufte, E. R. (1983). *The visual display of quantitative information.* Cheshire, CT: Graphics Press.

Wanderer, J. (1966). Academic origins of contributors to *American Sociological Review. American Sociologist, 1,* 241-243.

Wolins, L. (1962). Responsibility for raw data. *American Psychologist, 17,* 657-658.

About the Author

Bruce A. Thyer received his Ph.D. in social work and psychology from the University of Michigan in 1982. He holds appointments as Professor of Social Work and Adjunct Professor of Psychology at the University of Georgia and is Associate Clinical Professor of Psychiatry and Health Behavior at the Medical College of Georgia. He has published more than 125 articles in peer-reviewed journals in psychology, social work, and psychiatry; more than 25 book chapters in these fields; and six books. He is the editor of *Research on Social Work Practice,* a quarterly journal published by Sage Publications, and has served on the editorial boards of numerous journals. He also provides consultation and training to agencies and individuals interested in developing a program of professional publishing.